The EMOTIONAL CRAFT *of* FICTION

WRITER'S DIGEST
BOOKS

Writer's Digest Books
An imprint of Penguin Random House LLC
penguinrandomhouse.com

Printed in the United States of America

22nd Printing

ISBN 978-1-4403-4837-2

Edited by Cris Freese
Designed by Alexis Estoye

DEDICATION

For Margery Dowd Maass
my mother

ABOUT THE AUTHOR

Donald Maass founded the Donald Maass Literary Agency in New York in 1980. His agency sells more than 150 novels every year to major publishers in the U.S. and overseas. He is the author of *The Career Novelist* (1996), *Writing the Breakout Novel* (2001), *Writing the Breakout Novel Workbook* (2004), *The Fire in Fiction* (2009), *The Breakout Novelist* (2011), and *Writing 21st Century Fiction* (2012). He is a past president of the Association of Authors' Representatives, Inc.

TABLE OF CONTENTS

CHAPTER ONE

The EMOTIONAL CRAFT *of* FICTION

The world of fiction writers is a collection of opposites: factions at odds in their beliefs, values, purpose, and way of writing. Some authors have commercial intent; others, literary. Some outline; others explore story in successive drafts. For some, genre is a badge of pride; for others, it's a hateful label. Prestige matters greatly to some, money to others, and movie options to a misguided few.

A dichotomy less often discussed is the division between those who are comfortable writing emotions and those who find putting emotions on the page repellant. The latter group values *showing*. To get a reader to feel what a character feels, the thinking goes, put the reader through a character's experience. Provoke emotions in readers; don't spoon-feed them feelings. Most valuable of all to this group is the capturing of *moments*. These are passages so honest, vivid, and true that they transcend mere words. Readers recognize the universal human condition.

For other writers, *telling* is a positive. They go inside the mind and heart of a character to observe and feel story events just as that character does. Writing out characters' emotions is the essence of intimate storytelling. How else can you bring a character fully alive? For these authors, the highest expression of the art are passages of extended telling, in which a character's inward condition is captured in nuanced detail by means of words alone.

While few authors are purists of showing or telling, most lean more in one direction or the other. Even so, most agree that showing is better than telling, in general. And most blend the two. There isn't much debate of the topic. When it comes up at writer's conferences, the issue is usually framed as a question: *What's the right balance between showing and telling?*

Having researched, studied, and taught the handling of emotions in fiction, I have reached an altogether different conclusion. Fiction writers are asking the wrong question. Showing and telling are fine as far as they go, but the emotional experience of readers has little to do with that. The most useful question is not *how can I get across what characters are going through?* The better question is *how can I get readers to go on emotional journeys of their own?*

Showing and telling are only part of the picture. But, they are not even the most important part. As we will discover, readers may believe that they're living a story along with its characters. Actually, they're not. Readers are having their own experience that is merely occasioned by what's on the page.

That experience can be elicited, or not, by any number of story elements: plot, setting, theme, mood, dialogue, and, yes, what characters themselves feel. What the novelist is doing, though, is not causing readers to feel as the novelist does, or as his characters do, but rather inducing for each reader a unique emotional journey through a story. When you think about it, this makes perfect sense. No two readers read a novel the same way. How could they possibly? To see how differently folks experience a work of fiction, check their comments on Goodreads. Are those people all reading the same novel?

The purpose of this book is to delve into the ways and means of creating a powerful emotional experience for readers as they read. We'll look at effective ways of showing and telling, naturally, but there's much more to it than that. The dynamics of reader responses are complex. Equally complex and as varied in their effect are character arcs, journeys of self-discovery, which in turn cannot happen without ongoing emotional struggle.

The language of emotion in a novel also makes a difference to readers' experiences. Plot, too, can be understood as a sequence of emotional milestones. As a writer, you are on an emotional journey as you write, as well, a journey that informs and influences not only the story you are creating, but also your voice and very identity as a writer.

Why is it important to look at fiction writing through the lens of emotional experience? Because that's the way readers read. They don't so much read as *respond*. They do not automatically adopt your outlook and outrage. They formulate their own. You are not the author of what readers feel, just the provocateur of those feelings. You may curate your characters' experiences and put them on display, but the exhibit's meaning is different in thousands of ways for thousands of different museum visitors, your readers.

Not every published novel creates a powerful emotional experience for readers. In the slush pile the conditions are even worse. Too many manuscripts provoke very little feeling at all. The sad truth is that television commercials can stir more feelings in thirty seconds than many manuscripts do in three hundred pages.

How many novels have moved you to tears, rage, and a resolution to live differently? How many have left a permanent mark, branding you with a story that you will never forget? The number probably isn't great, and of that small number I suspect most of your memorable choices are not current novels but classics. What makes them classics? Artful storytelling, sure, but beyond the storytelling, classics have enduring appeal mostly because we remember the experiences we had while reading them; we remember not the art but the impact.

When a plot resolves, readers are satisfied, but what they remember of a novel is what they felt while reading it. Hooks may hook, twists may intrigue, tension may turn pages, and prose may dazzle, but all of those effects fade as quickly as fireworks in a night sky. Ask readers what they best remember about novels and most will say the characters, but is that accurate? It's true that characters become real to us but that is because of what they cause us to feel. Characters aren't actually real; only our own feelings are.

Emotional impact is not an extra. It's as fundamental to a novel's purpose and structure as its plot. The emotional craft of fiction underlies the creation of character arcs, plot turns, beginnings, midpoints, endings, and strong scenes. It is the basis of voice.

The emotional craft of fiction also can unlock the power of writing personally, reconnecting you to your story during those chaotic times when your novel falls to pieces and your sense of fun is gone. Emotional craft isn't a repackaging of old writing bromides. It's a way of understanding what causes emotional impact on readers and deliberately using those methods. It's a way to energize your writing with tools that are always available: your own feelings.

The methods in this book do not depend on plot formulas or scene checklists. They do not reduce the process to accidental discovery or luck. Being born with the unreliable gift of native genius won't help. Mastering the emotional craft of fiction starts with understanding how emotional impact is produced and then applying that in practice.

It isn't magic, but the results will feel magical. The mastery of this craft will not change your story type, style, or intent. It doesn't matter whether you're commercial or literary; pantsing or plotting; or working in a genre, mashing genres up, or blazing a trail. All manuscripts, as I said, need to make readers feel more, and the methods for doing that are set out for you here.

I have already written several successful books on fiction craft, so why this new approach? What makes it different? Why is it better? Why is it even necessary? For me emotional craft became a necessary study because I realized that in reading many manuscripts, and also published novels, I was feeling little. The high action of best-selling thrillers often left me cold. Speculative fiction engaged my imagination but did not often touch my soul. Romance and women's fiction wallowed in feelings but frequently left me feeling indifferent.

Literary fiction can be the driest reading experience of all. Beautiful writing may sparkle like a diamond necklace, but sparkling isn't a feeling. The greatest wish of editors today is a strong *voice*, and that's fine, but even strong voices can fail to reach my heart. Strong writing doesn't automatically produce strong feelings. Paradoxically, poorly written novels can sometimes unsettle me, stir me to anger, or send me reaching for a tissue.

I want to feel more as I read. Don't you? That's why this book and the methods herein matter. When readers feel strongly, their hearts are open. Your stories can not only reach them for a moment, but they can change them forever. I don't care about what you write, how you write it, your choices in publishing, or what you want out of your career. What I want is to feel deeply as I read your work. I want to feel connected to you and your characters in the way I do to the most memorable classics and the most stunning new titles I'll read this year.

Does that goal sound good to you? I hope so. The pages ahead are a guide for how to get there.

CHAPTER TWO

INNER *versus* OUTER

There are three primary paths to producing an emotional response in readers. The first is to report what characters are feeling so effectively that readers feel something too. This is *inner mode*, the telling of emotions. As though talking with friends over coffee, we nod, furrow our brows, gasp, protest, wonder, and ask questions as if the character's feelings were our own.

The second is to provoke in readers what characters may be feeling by implying their inner state through external action. This is *outer mode*, the showing of emotions. Like billiard balls colliding, the theory goes, a character's actions transfer an emotional impact to

the reader, who feels it with equal force, and the reader caroms across the table. There's no description of the feeling; we simply roll with it.

The third method is to cause readers to feel something that a story's characters do not themselves feel. This is *other mode*, an emotional dialogue between author and reader. The reader reacts, resists, and sometimes succumbs, but thanks to the author's skill, she can never escape the churn and flow of her own feelings.

All three paths to producing emotional responses in readers are valid, but all three have pitfalls and can fail to work. To successfully use each, it's necessary to understand why each is effective when it is. Once you know the underlying cause behind the surface effects, you'll know whether the approach that you are taking on a given page will reliably move readers' hearts.

OUTER MODE: SHOWING

The choice between inner and outer modes is a central one. Some story types, such as romance fiction, necessarily rely on inner mode. Others, like thrillers, either have no time to dwell on characters' feelings or their authors regard such passages as artless and possibly repellant.

Writers of women's fiction are caught in the middle. Given this story type and its audience, you'd think this wouldn't be much of an issue. In women's fiction it's the inner experience of characters that we want to read, right? Changes and growth *are* the story. A journey of transformation is mostly taken inside, so inner mode would seem to be the default mode of choice.

On the other hand, women's fiction writers usually hope to do more than entertain. Their fiction may be warm, fun, and loaded with chocolate and recipes, but it's also serious. It has something to say. It ought to be well written, for how else will you win starred reviews and hope to raise questions for book clubs to discuss? Such artfulness requires showing.

Yet outer moments in many manuscripts can feel small and self-consciously "written"; in other words, arty more than artful. How can that be? Nothing is more valid and vivid than what we can see and hear, right? Human action is also driven by need. That need is sensed in subtext and revealed through what people say and do. That in turn should stir our own imaginations and churn up our feelings, shouldn't it?

That's not really true. When outward actions stir us, it's not the actions we read that have stirred us but that we have stirred ourselves. Action is an opportunity for us to feel something, not a cause of feeling something. The distinction matters. It explains that when showing works the thing we should look at is not *why* it works but *when*.

Matthew Quick's *The Silver Linings Playbook* (2008) is a novel featuring a protagonist, Pat Peoples, who is certifiably crazy. Pat begins the novel in a neural health facility, from which he is released with the help of his mother. Quick knows the trick of making a mentally ill protagonist enjoyable to read about: Make him funny. Pat Peoples amusingly refuses to give up his dream of reuniting with his estranged wife, Nikki, and is convinced that their "apart time," as he calls it, will end. All evidence is to the contrary, of course, as we see when Pat returns home:

> When I finally come out of the basement, I notice that all the pictures of Nikki and me have been removed from the walls and the mantel over the fireplace.
>
> I ask my mother where these pictures went. She tells me our house was burglarized a few weeks before I came home and the pictures were stolen. I ask why a burglar would want pictures of Nikki and me, and my mother says she puts all of her pictures in very expensive frames. "Why didn't the burglar steal the rest of the family pictures?" I ask. Mom says the burglar stole all the expensive frames, but she had the negatives for the family portraits and had them replaced. "Why didn't you replace the pictures of Nikki

and me?" I ask. Mom says she did not have the negatives for the pictures of Nikki and me, especially because Nikki's parents had paid for the wedding pictures and had only given my mother copies of the photos she liked. Nikki had given Mom the other non-wedding pictures of us, and well, we aren't in touch with Nikki or her family right now because it's apart time.

Notice that Quick does not try to convey what Pat is feeling in this farcical passage. There's no need. Pat's delusional refusal to accept that Nikki is not coming back to him is plainly evident. This objective, wry, reportorial approach serves Quick's purpose well because if we were asked to swallow the inner emotional life of Pat Peoples, we couldn't. It's too crazy and painful.

This is demonstrated again in the next chapter when Pat, to fulfill a condition of his release, goes for his first appointment with his outside psychiatrist, Dr. Cliff Patel:

> As I sit there flipping through a *Sports Illustrated*, listening to the easy-listening station Dr. Patel pumps into his waiting room, suddenly I'm hearing sexy synthesizer chords, faint high-hat taps, the kick drum thumping out an erotic heartbeat, the twinkling of fairy dust, and then the evil bright soprano saxophone. You know the title: "Songbird." And I'm out of my seat, screaming, kicking chairs, flipping the coffee table, picking up piles of magazines and throwing them against the wall, yelling, "It's not fair! I won't tolerate any tricks! I'm not an emotional lab rat!"
>
> And then a small Indian man—maybe only five feet tall, wearing a cable-knit sweater in August, suit pants, and shiny white tennis shoes—is calmly asking me what's wrong.
>
> "Turn off that music!" I yell. "Shut if off! Right now!"
>
> The tiny man is Dr. Patel, I realize, because he tells his secretary to turn off the music, and when she obeys, Kenny G is out of my head and I stop yelling.
>
> I cover my face with my hands so no one will see my crying, and after a minute or so, my mother begins rubbing my back.

So much silence—and then Dr. Patel asks me into his office. I follow him reluctantly as Mom helps the secretary clean up the mess I made.

His office is pleasantly strange.

What is Pat feeling? Quick doesn't report that because it doesn't matter. What matters is what readers feel, which perhaps is shock, horror, or even compassion for a guy who obviously is in distress. (I find Kenny G's greatest hits somewhat saccharine, I'll admit, but hardly a reason to overturn coffee tables.)

Showing is all that's needed here. That's important to remember if your characters are dark, tormented, suffering, or insane. The painful emotional lives of such characters need to become tolerable for readers. Humor and objective showing create a safety zone. In that zone readers can process their own response to emotional conditions that are extreme.

To put it simply, when character emotions are highly painful, pull back.

One secret ingredient behind effective showing can be summed up in this word: *subtext*. When there's a feeling we're not being told, but it is evident anyway, that underlying feeling is the subtext. It's the unspoken emotional truth. When we discern it, it's a surprise.

The opening of Gregory David Roberts's *The Mountain Shadow* (2015), his sequel to *Shantaram* (2003), would seem to have plenty to surprise readers with—a mix of mysticism, crime, and romance, as well as its setting, the slums of Bombay. However, Roberts uses subtext in small ways throughout to keep us wondering about that which we aren't being told.

In this early passage of dialogue, Roberts's Australian fugitive hero, Lin, is walking away from an opium den and talking with two acquaintances: Vikram, for whom he has recently (and violently) reclaimed from a loan shark a necklace belonging to Vikram's mother, and Naveen, a would-be detective. They are the kind of close friends that only people who share criminal records can be.

> [Vikram] was about to step into the taxi but I stopped him, leaning in close to speak quietly.
>
> "What are you doing?"
>
> "What do you mean?"
>
> "You can't lie to me about drugs, Vik."
>
> "What lying!" he protested. "Shit, I just had a few puffs of brown sugar, that's all. So what? It's Concannon's stuff, anyway. He paid for it. I—"
>
> "Take it easy."
>
> "I always take it easy. You know me."
>
> "Some people can snap out of a habit, Vikram. Concannon might be one of them. You're not one of them. You know that."
>
> He smiled, and for a few seconds the old Vikram was there: the Vikram who would've gone to Goa for the necklace without any help from me, or anyone else; the Vikram who wouldn't have left a piece of his mother's wedding jewelry with a loan shark in the first place.
>
> The smile folded from his eyes as he got into the taxi. I watched him away, worried for the danger in what he was: an optimist, ruined by love.
>
> I started walking again, and Naveen fell in beside me.
>
> "He talks about that girl, the English girl, a lot," Naveen said.
>
> "It's one of those things that should've worked out, but rarely do."
>
> "He talks about you a lot, too," Naveen said.
>
> "He talks too much."
>
> "He talks about Karla and Didier and Lisa. But mostly he talks about you."
>
> "He talks too much."
>
> "He told me that you escaped from prison," he said. "And that you're on the run."
>
> I stopped walking.
>
> "Now you're talking too much. What is this, an epidemic?"

Whoa, what's up with Lin? There's something about him we don't know and that he'd obviously prefer we didn't. What does he feel? He isn't saying, but that's not important, or anyway it's less important than what *we* feel when he abruptly turns on Naveen.

So what do we feel? First of all, the moment is nicely set up for a reversal. Lin cares enough about Vikram to caution him about drug use, which Vikram is prone to because of his sorrow over a lost love. However, it is Lin who has the more dangerous criminal tendencies. (He also has a lost love, his soul mate, Karla, who is now married to a handsome Indian media tycoon.) When Naveen mentions Lin's fugitive status, Lin goes on high alert. So do we. We don't know what Lin feels, but we know what we feel: *Watch out!*

The previous passage is a tiny passing moment in the opening of *The Mountain Shadow*, but this little jolt of discovery, of subtext, of showing, both gives us a shiver and contributes to an accretion of emotional splashes that, like waves, grow into a tsunami of tragic proportions. Lin's story of must-go-can't-leave-Bombay plays out with emotional force, but oftentimes that force is stealthy, sneaky, and unseen. Small doses of subtext sum up to a big effect.

Showing isn't necessarily limited to external action or dialogue, or that which we can see or hear. Situations and conditions such as a state of being can be presented without emotions and, despite that, cause us to feel quite a bit. Examples of this can be found throughout the work of the Grand Master of Showing, Ernest Hemingway. His take on fiction technique was simple:

> Find what gave you the emotion; what the action was that gave you the excitement. Then write it down making it clear so the reader will see it too and have the same feeling as you had.

There you have it, the pithy advice left to us by one of the greatest writers of the twentieth century. It sounds simple, and indeed when Hemingway followed his own advice the results were gripping.

Here's the opening paragraph of Hemingway's short story "Now I Lay Me":

> That night we lay on the floor in the room and I listened to the silk-worms eating. The silk-worms fed in racks of mulberry leaves and all night you could hear them eating and a dropping sound in the leaves. I myself did not want to sleep because I had been living for a long time with the knowledge that if I ever shut my eyes in the dark and let myself go, my soul would go out of my body. I had been that way for a long time, ever since I had been blown up at night and felt it go out of me and go off and then come back. I tried never to think about it, but it had started to go since, in the nights, just at the moment of going off to sleep, and I could only stop it by a very great effort. So while I am now fairly sure that it would not really have gone out, yet then, that summer, I was unwilling to make the experiment.

Note the type of showing that Hemingway is using. This isn't action, *per se*. This is the inner state of a man suffering from sleeplessness. He's a victim of shell shock, now called post-traumatic stress disorder. He recalls an out-of-body experience, something that Hemingway himself experienced in World War I.

What about Hemingway's style? Is it literary? Hardly. Not with all that plain language and those clunky compound sentences. Not a fancy word in sight, either. Imagery? The gnawing silkworms are unusual. They provide the intrigue that at the outset hooks us into his story.

Now, as you read that passage, what do you feel? For me the passage is plain, even awkward, yet arresting. What I feel is something like compassion, quiet horror, and helplessness rolled up into one. There is suffering. This is a soldier burdened by the aftereffects of war. The terror of the out-of-body experience he underwent gnaws at him as surely as the silkworms gnaw at the leaves.

Hemingway's passage does not tell you what the point-of-view character feels. As Hemingway intended, he merely creates the experience, and we in turn feel something. But here's the thing: The experience that Hemingway creates is not a mundane day-to-day washing of dishes or making tea. It's not just any garden-variety insomnia. This ex-soldier is haunted by a brush with death itself.

Hemingway did not ask us to be gripped by domestic trivialities. He wrote about big stuff. And that's my point. Lying awake at night is not by itself going to cause readers to feel anything. Only when a situation has heavy emotional baggage will readers pick up that baggage and carry it.

But what about small stuff, you may be asking. How do some authors entrance us with what seems mundane?

Good question.

Anthony Doerr's bestseller *All the Light We Cannot See* (2014) emphatically is a literary novel. Doerr places high value on language, imagery, and moments. Looked at structurally, it's like a collection of literary postcards. It's not built of scenes that enact change so much as moments with meaning, slices of reality that illuminate the condition of his characters.

The novel is set during World War II but circles back to the 1930s and the earlier lives of Doerr's two protagonists, a young German soldier and a blind French girl. The girl, Marie-Laure, grows up in Paris, where her father works in a museum of natural history. Stored in this museum is a diamond that is said to be cursed. As the museum prepares to put this diamond on display, superstition and anxiety run rampant. In this passage, a colleague of Marie-Laure's father tries to reassure her:

> Dr. Geffard's answers are hardly better. "You know how diamonds—how all crystals—grow, Laurette? By adding microscopic layers, a few thousand atoms every month, each atop the next. Millennia after millennia. That's how stories accumulate too. All the old

stones accumulate stories. That little rock you're so curious about may have seen Alaric sack Rome; it may have glittered in the eyes of Pharaohs. Scythian queens might have danced all night wearing it. Wars might have been fought over it."

"Papa says curses are only stories cooked up to deter thieves. He says there are sixty-five million specimens in this place, and if you have the right teacher, each can be as interesting as the last."

"Still," he says, "certain things compel people. Pearls, for example and sinistral shells, shells with a left-hand opening. Even the best scientists feel the urge now and then to put something in a pocket. That something so small could be so beautiful. Worth so much. Only the strongest people can turn away from feelings like that."

They are quiet for a moment.

Marie-Laure says, "I heard that a diamond is like a piece of light from the original world. Before it fell. A piece of light rained to earth from God."

"You want to know what it looks like. That's why you're so curious."

She rolls a murex in her hands. Holds it to her ear. Ten thousand drawers, ten thousand whispers inside ten thousand shells.

"No," she said. "I want to believe that Papa hasn't been anywhere near it."

Squint and you'd almost think that Doerr is writing about literary fiction: *That something so small could be so beautiful. ...only the strongest people can turn away from feelings like that.* Actually, Doerr is writing about museum specimens. The passage is packed with sparkling imagery. Gems. Geology. Curses. So how does that imagery itself cause us to feel? It doesn't. It can't. What causes us to feel something is a blind daughter's worry over her father.

Pearls and sistral shells? Pretty images, yes, but not as effective as a single, strong feeling.

EMOTIONAL MASTERY 1: EFFECTIVE SHOWING

- Select a moment in your story when your protagonist is moved, unsettled, or disturbed. This might occur when he's facing a difficult choice, needing something badly, suffering a setback or surprise, having a self-realization, learning something shocking, or feeling in any way overwhelmed. Write down all the emotions inherent in this moment, both obvious and hidden.
- Next, considering what he is feeling, write down how your protagonist can act out. What is the biggest thing your protagonist can do? What would be explosive, out of bounds, or offensive? What would be symbolic? What can your protagonist say that would cut right to the heart of the matter or unite others in understanding? Go sideways, underneath, or ahead. How can your protagonist show us a feeling that we don't expect to see?
- Add a detail of the setting that only your protagonist would notice, or that everyone notices but your protagonist sees in a unique way.
- Finally, go back and delete all the emotions you wrote down at the beginning of this exercise. Let actions and spoken words do the work. Do they feel too big, dangerous, or over-the-top? Use them anyway. Others will tell you if you've gone too far, but more likely, you haven't gone far enough.

By the way, before we leave Hemingway, it's often said that he hated writing about emotions. That's not wholly true. He could brilliantly capture pure emotion, as he did in this passage from his story "In Another Country," which concerns a soldier undergoing rehabilitation in a hospital in Milan for an injury to his knee. Several other-wounded Italian soldiers are also undergoing treatment:

> The boys at first were very polite about my medals and asked me what I had done to get them. I showed them the papers, which were written in very beautiful language and full of fratellanza and abnegazione, but which really said, with the adjectives removed,

that I had been given the medals because I was an American. After that their manner changed a little toward me, although I was their friend against outsiders. I was a friend, but I was never really one of them after they had read the citations, because it had been different with them and they had done very different things to get their medals. I had been wounded, it was true; but we all knew that being wounded, after all, was really an accident. I was never ashamed of the ribbons, though, and sometimes, after the cocktail hour, I would imagine myself having done all the things they had done to get their medals; but walking home at night through the empty streets and with the cold wind and all the shops closed, trying to keep near the street lights, I knew that I would never have done such things, and that I was very much afraid to die, and often lay in bed at night by myself, afraid to die and wondering how I would be when I went back to the front again.

"Afraid to die." You don't get much more direct than that. Direct and plain emotions stated like this don't often have a strong effect, but they do in this case, I think, because we're already gripped by an earlier, unspoken emotion: shame. That has opened us up, put us in an emotional groove. The blunt sentiment "afraid to die" then hits like a cymbal crash at the end of a measure.

When showing has an impact it is because the action is freighted with feelings in the first place. You're probably not going to get much emotional mileage out of pouring a bowl of cereal, tidying up the house, or in other ways portraying everyday realism. When that does work, it's because large emotions are already there.

INNER MODE: TELLING

Writing out what characters feel ought to be a shortcut to getting readers to feel that stuff too, shouldn't it? You'd think so. After all, it's through characters that we experience a story. Their experience is ours. Actually, the truth is the opposite. Put on the page what a character feels and there's a pretty good chance that, paradoxically, what the reader will feel is nothing.

Here's an example: *His guts twisted in fear.* When you read that, do your own guts twist in fear? Probably not. Or this: *Her eyes shot daggers at him.* Do you feel simmering rage? Meh. Not so much.

Such feelings fail to excite us because, of course, we've read them too many times. Those daggers have dulled. What gets readers going are feelings that are fresh and unexpected. Yet those feelings also need to be real and true; otherwise, they will come across as contrived—they'll ring false and fail to ignite the reader's emotions.

Skillful authors play against expected feelings. They go down several emotional layers in order to bring up emotions that will catch readers by surprise. There's always a different emotion to use. A story situation is an emotional elephant. There are many ways of looking at and feeling about what's happening at any given moment. Stop your story at any point, ask the point-of-view character what she is feeling, and it's never just one answer. Ask two characters what they feel about what's happening and neither will ever say the same thing.

Human beings are complex. We have emotions on the surface and emotions underneath. There are emotions that we minimize, hide, and deny. There are emotions that embarrass us, reveal too much, and make us vulnerable. Our emotions can be profoundly trivial or so elevated that they're silly. What we feel is inescapably influenced by our history, morals, loyalties, and politics.

Our feelings are also communal. We pick up on others. We can project feelings that are mean, selfish, and destructive onto others. We can reserve feelings that are noble, selfless, and bold for ourselves. We laugh at funerals and cry at weddings.

We're clear. We're vague. We hate. We love. We feel passionately about our shoes yet shrug off disasters on TV. We are finely tuned sensors of right and wrong, and horrible examples for our kids. We are walking contradictions. We are encyclopedias of the heart.

Our feelings are also dynamic. They change. They can reverse in an instant. We can be torn, confused, and frustrated, which only means that our feelings are in conflict. We can be stuck, shut down, apathetic, or a mess. We can be dead inside or newly alive. We experience awakenings, self-awareness, hope, and joy.

With so much rich human material to work with, it's disappointing to me that so many manuscripts offer a limited menu of emotions. I want to feast on life, but instead I'm standing before a fast-food menu, my choices limited to two patties or one, fries medium or large. That is to say, I see a menu of simple, primary emotions. Other manuscripts show off, strive for effect, or so wildly elaborate characters' feelings that I feel like a visitor at a gallery of impenetrable modern art. I can't connect.

The feelings that writers first choose to write are often obvious, easy, and safe. These are the feelings writers believe they *ought* to use if their stories are going to sell. They work only with primary emotions because that is what everyone feels, which is true, but this is also a limited view.

So how does one create emotional surprise? Is it possible to be both artful and accessible? Can emotions feel right and connect with us even when we don't see them coming? Certainly.

Let's start with an example from a master of secondary emotions: Ray Bradbury. In *Fahrenheit 451*, Guy Montag is a futuristic fireman who burns books. He enjoys his job until he meets a seventeen-year-old girl who awakens his mind. After his transformation begins he's called to help burn a house full of books, and Montag secretly takes one. The house and its contents are then doused with kerosene. The woman who lives in the house is warned to leave but refuses and holds up ...

> An ordinary kitchen match.
>
> The sight of it rushed the men out and down away from the house. Captain Beatty, keeping his dignity, backed slowly through

the front door, his pink face burnt and shiny from a thousand fires and night excitements. God, thought Montag, how true! Always at night the alarm comes. Never by day! Is it because fire is prettier by night? More spectacle, a better show? The pink face of Beatty now showed the faintest panic in the door. The woman's hand twitched on the single matchstick. The fumes of kerosene bloomed up about her. Montag felt the hidden book pound like a heart against his chest.

A careless writer would have focused on Montag's horror at what was about to happen. *No! Don't do it!* Bradbury, however, knows that the obvious emotion will not have the desired effect. Instead he portrays a feeling that we don't expect: Montag's excitement.

Excitement? Remember that Montag is a fireman who has enjoyed starting fires. He knows the thrill of watching books burn. The expression on the face of his chief, Beatty, ignites that feeling again, briefly, even while Montag's heart is changing. Because Bradbury goes sideways from an expected feeling, we cannot help but feel something ourselves. In this horrific situation we are forced to measure Montag's emotion against our own. How can we not? Is his excitement what we would feel? No. Or maybe yes, if we were Montag.

Bradbury wasn't the first to figure this out. Literary greats like Hardy, Wharton, Forsyth, Lawrence, and many others knew that writing about emotions is as necessary and narrative as writing about anything else. They also understood that to be effective, writing about emotions has to be artful, which is another way of saying surprising.

One of Daphne Du Maurier's less often read, but eminently worthwhile, novels is *My Cousin Rachel* (1951), which is about young and headstrong Philip Ashley, who has been raised by his beloved cousin Ambrose, a confirmed bachelor. When, for health reasons, Ambrose must winter in Italy, Philip is devastated but must stay behind to manage Ambrose's estate, which he will presumably someday inherit. All is miserable in Ambrose's absence, and then comes an even greater blow: a letter breaking to Philip the news that Ambrose has met, fallen in love with, and married a distant cousin of theirs, the vivacious but mysterious Rachel.

Du Maurier plays the moment this way:

> The letter came about half-past five, just after I had dined. Luckily, I was alone. Seecombe had brought in the post-bag, and left it with me. I put the letter in my pocket and walked out across the fields down to the sea. Seecombe's nephew, who had the mill cottage on the beach, said good-day to me. He had his nets spread on the stone wall, drying in the last of the sun. I barely answered him, and he must have thought me curt. I climbed over the rocks to a narrow ledge, jutting into the little bay, where I used to swim in summer. Ambrose would anchor some fifty yards out in his boat, and I would swim to him. I sat down, and taking the letter from my pocket read it again. If I could have felt one spark of sympathy, of gladness, one single ray of warmth towards those two who were sharing happiness together down in Naples, it would have eased my conscience. Ashamed of myself, bitterly angry at my selfishness, I could raise no feeling in my heart at all. I sat there, numb with misery, staring at the flat calm sea. I had just turned twenty-three, and yet I felt as lonely and as lost as I had done years before, sitting on a bench in Fourth Form, at Harrow, with no one to befriend me, and nothing before me, only a new world of strange experience that I did not want.

Philip's selfish misery at Ambrose's news would be hard to take. Why isn't it? Philip is ashamed of himself. He knows he should feel happy for Ambrose and Rachel but cannot find a shred of gladness in his heart. Nevertheless, there is no other way to feel. He is once again an orphan—abandoned by his caretaker and sent away to boarding school. It is a lonely experience.

What word would you use to describe Philip's inner state? Miserable? Bereft? Abandoned? Of those three, only the first word is used in the passage. Even so, the totality of Philip's emotional state is more than the sum of its parts. How does Du Maurier do that?

First there is the deft metaphor for Philip's lost security: his memory of swimming to the safety of Ambrose's boat. Even more devastating is Philip's memory of sitting alone at Harrow. Du Maurier also gives Philip a moral judgment about himself: He is ashamed of his lack of empathy. Finally, he feels justified in this feeling, or at any rate, helpless in the face of his feelings.

In other words, Du Maurier does not stop with *I felt miserable*, the obvious emotion. She digs deeper. She uses a metaphor (the swimming memory) and an analogy for Philip's inner state (lonely on a bench at Harrow). She lists alternative feelings that Philip might feel (sympathy, gladness, happiness). She, or rather Philip, makes a moral judgment about his feelings (shame), and Philip feels justified in his feelings.

To sum it up, here are the four steps of Du Maurier's emotional method: 1) an analogy, 2) alternatives, 3) moral judgment, and 4) justification. Rather than simply saying what Phillip feels, Du Maurier gives us a discourse on the emotional possibilities and why there are no real alternatives to what he feels.

EMOTIONAL MASTERY 2: THIRD-LEVEL EMOTIONS

- Select any moment in your story when your protagonist feels something strongly. Identify the feeling. Next, ask your protagonist, "What else are you feeling at this moment?" Write that down, too. Then ask, "Okay, what else are you feeling now?" Write that down.
- Now begin to work with that third, lower-layer emotion. Examine it in four ways. 1) Objectify it by creating an analogy: What does it feel like to have this feeling? 2) Make a moral judgment about it: Is it good or bad to feel this? Why? 3) Create an alternative: What would a better person feel instead?

4) Justify this feeling: It's the only possible thing to feel at this moment and here is why.
- Look around the scene, too. What is your protagonist seeing that others don't? Add one detail that only your protagonist would see, and see it in his own unique way.
- Write a new passage for this moment in the story, one in which your character feels deeply (and in detail) this third-level emotion.

An important part of this method is the lengthy discourse that I mentioned. Why delve so deeply? One reason is to create a longer passage for the reader. That in turn creates a period of time, perhaps fifteen seconds, for the reader's brain to process. That interval is necessary. It gives readers the opportunity to arrive at their own emotional response, a response that we cannot know.

Or can we? Ah. Here's where things get interesting. Let's take the common feeling (in stories, at least) of fear. It's all but impossible to write about fear and get readers to feel it. In workshops, though, I ask participants to find a moment when a character feels afraid. We then drill down and develop a third-level emotion in the ways suggested above. When the resulting passages are read, other participants report feeling … guess what?

Fear.

That's how it works. Be obvious and tell readers what to feel, and they won't feel it. Light an unexpected match, though, and readers will ignite their own feelings, which may well prove to be the ones that are primary and obvious. Third-level emotions. That's the effective way of telling.

OTHER MODE

As I've said, none of readers' emotional experience of a story actually comes from the emotional lives of characters. It comes from readers themselves. Yes, showing and telling are part of what provokes readers to feel, but they are only a part. Other things on the page also provoke readers, and these things are the greater part of the equation.

It might seem that you shouldn't worry about what readers feel; they're either going to feel what you want them to feel or not. But that way of thinking surrenders too much to chance. It leads to the erroneous idea that emotional effect is accidental. While it's true that you cannot control what each reader will feel while reading your work, what you can control is whether they will feel something in the first place and how strong those feelings will be.

What is actually happening inside readers as they read? Each reader has a unique emotional response to a story. It's unpredictable but it's real. Readers read under the influence of their own temperaments, histories, biases, morality, likes, dislikes, and peeves. They make judgments that don't agree with yours. So how can a writer predict, never mind control, what readers feel?

Psychological research can help us, to a point. Research shows that consumers of entertainment are seeking, more than anything, to have an experience. That should come as no surprise. Does "an experience" sound simplistic? Yes, but it's also important. An experience, sure, but what *kind* of experience? Research shows this: Readers expect their experience, naturally enough, to be a positive one.

Positive means feeling enjoyment, suspense, amusement, and the satisfaction of what psychologists call *belief affirmation*— stories turning out as readers believe they should. That requires more than just a happy ending. It means affirming readers' beliefs and validating their morals. But is that what authors want, too? Sometimes, but not always.

Authors want to challenge readers. Research shows that readers want this, too.

Entertainment gives consumers feelings of competence, autonomy, and relatedness. Let's break those down. *Competence* comes from mastering the challenges presented in a story. Literary readers

THE EMOTIONAL CRAFT OF FICTION

especially like to be challenged, to a point. *Autonomy* means that readers feel unique in their reading choices, which of course isn't exactly true given that so many consumers buy bestsellers. *Relatedness* comes from the adoration of characters, which is explained by *affective disposition theory*, discussed in chapter five.

There's more research that supports authors' intentions to provoke readers. Entertainment works best when it presents consumers with novelty, challenge, and aesthetic value, which in turn cause *cognitive evaluation*. In plain language that means thinking, guessing, questioning, and comparing what is happening to one's own experience. Medically speaking, this is actually necessary for human health and well-being. When readers chew on a story, they are getting not only what they want, but also something good and healthy.

This *chewing effect* has another benefit: Readers are more likely to remember a story when it has made them chew. That's because memory is not just one thing. What we read is first processed in *sensory memory*, our immediate experience of it. Processing then moves to *working memory*, the place where we do the chewing. The longer stuff stays in working memory, the more likely it is to be boxed and shrink-wrapped by our *episode buffers* and swallowed into *long-term memory*, the place from which we recall things.

What all that means is that readers fundamentally want to feel something, not about your story, but about themselves. They want to play. They want to anticipate, guess, think, and judge. They want to finish a story and feel competent. They want to feel like they've been through something. They want to connect with your characters and live their fictional experience, or believe that they have.

Creating that type of experience for readers requires more than just walking them through the plot. Feeling can be induced by plot developments, but only to a limited extent. Plot *per se* intrigues, excites, and surprises us, or so we hope, but not much more than that.

As we've seen, characters' emotional states also, by themselves, are limited in their impact.

The emotional wallop of a story is created by its totality. Readers experience that wallop when they must not just form an opinion about a story, but when they must study, question, and form an opinion about *themselves*. Simply put, they want to—they *must*—take an emotional journey.

Other mode is not a single technique or principle. It is a vast array of elements tuned like the instruments in an orchestra to create a soaring emotional effect. When all the instruments work together, they lift our hearts. They transport us to a realm of wonder. We are open.

Do you hope that your fiction can change people or maybe even history? Your hope is not in vain. It actually can. That power, however, cannot exist unless and until a story has a strong emotional impact. So how do you achieve that impact? The answer to that question is the subject of the rest of this book.

CHAPTER THREE

The EMOTIONAL WORLD

Dive from a high platform, walk a country lane, watch your computer freeze, cross a finish line, hear your morning alarm, look for a parking space, toast on your anniversary, embrace a friend after a funeral. As you live your life, what do you feel? Terror, serenity, frustration, relief, groaning reluctance, patient endurance, pride, satisfaction, or a grief made bearable because somehow life will go on.

We experience life as feelings. It's funny, then, that so much fiction is written to minimize feelings or leave them out altogether. It's as if emotions are not a fit subject or writing about them is too simplistic. Even fiction that celebrates feelings, romance for instance, can sometimes work with only a limited and familiar emotional palette. We can wallow in emotional content yet feel curiously empty.

It doesn't have to be that way.

The emotional experience of a story, both for characters and for readers, can be far richer than it often is. Authors would like that to be true, but how can that be achieved without bogging things down or boring readers with the obvious? When the mandate is to keep things visual, exciting, external, and changing, how are you supposed to spend page time on what is amorphous, internal, reflective, and static? Emotions aren't story.

Despite that, great storytellers are able to make emotions as compelling as anything else on the page. They make the emotional life of characters the focus rather than a sideshow. They make familiar emotions fresh and small feelings large. They immerse us in the emotional worlds of characters without indulging in darkness or sickening us in the sun. They stir the high human emotions that make stories memorable.

How? Here are some fiction elements that do not by themselves elicit emotion: voice, closely written point of view, and imagery. Voice grabs our attention. Intimate point of view gives us the "as if" illusion of temporarily being someone else. Deft imagery makes an imaginary place startlingly real. All fine. All necessary. None of it emotional.

So what is emotional on the page? Let's take a look at the methods that make us feel as we read.

ME-CENTERED NARRATION

"Let's talk about me!"

Generally speaking, that's not a great idea for handling yourself in social situations. A better plan is to listen and ask questions. Being interested in others is the way to make friends and influence people. In bonding readers to characters on the page, however, the reverse is true. We open our hearts to those whose hearts are first open to us.

For characters' hearts to be open to readers, characters must talk to us quite a bit about what's going on inside. In many manuscripts, the characters don't disclose much. Often they, or rather their authors, simply report what's happening to them—a dry, play-by-play conveyance of the action. Even the witty, ironically detached first-person voices of Young Adult, New Adult, and Para-Everything fiction aren't necessarily open. An ironic, snarky, or perky tone can be used to avoid true intimacy with readers. Literary writing isn't necessarily intimate, either. A life "closely observed" doesn't mean we'll care about it.

Elsewhere I have advocated building the world of the story not by describing how it looks, sounds, feels, smells, or tastes, but rather by conveying characters' experience of that world. Opening the emotional world of a story is just as important, but doing so involves delving not only into characters' experience of their world but also of themselves.

For some authors this can be uncomfortable. Plot-driven storytellers, for example, may fear that they're slowing the action. Character-driven storytellers can be afraid of getting their characters' inner lives wrong, believing that even a tiny misstep can ruin years of effort. Both fears strangle emotional effect. The truth is that there is nothing wrong with opening up characters' inner lives. The bigger problem is that most authors don't do so enough. That said, letting characters simply gush on the page isn't terribly effective, either.

Creating a world that is emotionally involving for readers means raising questions and concerns about that world. It means both welcoming readers inside that world and making them curious, or uneasy, about where they are. First-person narration, the self-absorbed voice of our age, would seem to do that automatically but that belief is deceptive. True emotional engagement happens when a reader isn't just enjoying a character's patter but when she cannot avoid self-reflection, whether she's aware of it happening or not.

What provokes readers to experience their own profound sense of self? How do readers feel their oats, pick up their own baggage, smile at their own ironies, snap out of their worries, and feel that things today actually are okay? In life, things like that can happen when we bounce off of others or pick up the moods of others. We lock horns, back away from bias, scream at rock concerts, cheer at football games, nod in agreement, join the mob and pick up stones to throw, or raise our palms to heaven and murmur an amen. The effect is similar in fiction. In reading fiction we react to what others are feeling strongly, in this case the characters. Strong feelings are an invitation. Or a challenge. Strong feelings press us to judge what characters feel. We sympathize with them, or not. We engage on our own level.

Novels would not seem to have much in common with pop songs, rap, and Broadway show tunes, but there is a song topic that on the page also nicely provokes us. It's the song that declares, "I Am." You're probably familiar with Bob Dylan's version of "I Am a Man of Constant Sorrow," a folk tune that goes way back. Think of Helen Reddy's feminist anthem "I Am Woman" or Simon and Garfunkel's "I Am a Rock," or, absurdly, John Lennon's "I Am the Walrus." These songs make a declarative statement about self.

Characters can do the same on the page, but it's important to see that simple chest pounding is not the point. The purpose of an "I am" passage is not to declare something true but to cause readers to suspect that what's being forcefully asserted might, in fact, be false.

Diane Setterfield followed the success of her neo-Gothic novel *The Thirteenth Tale* (2006) with the cautionary fable *Bellman & Black* (2013), about the spooky rise and fall of Victorian entrepreneur William Bellman, who as a boy killed a rook with a slingshot. Don't mess with rooks. They don't forget, or die. Bellman is haunted by a mysterious stranger in black (dubbed Mr. Black, naturally enough), whose periodic appearance in his life correlates with tragedy, but also opportunity.

It is Mr. Black whom Bellman believes has given him the idea of creating London's largest millinery focused on mourning, Bellman & Black. Everything the shop sells is black. It will become hugely successful. As the emporium readies to open, Bellman feels invigorated and highly pleased with himself, for the most part.

How vast London was. How great the extent of its housing and commerce and population. There was not a living soul in this city, not so far as the eye could see, that would not at some point have need of the goods and services provided by Bellman & Black. He looked out, turning slowly, in all directions. Birds were swooping and diving in the darkening sky, and beneath them, streets of houses stretched in all directions, grand and modest and impoverished. In one of those houses, in Richmond say, a fellow would be sneezing, right at this very moment. Just as in Mayfair someone was shivering. In Spitalfields, a tainted oyster was slipping down someone's throat, and in Bloomsbury someone was pouring the glass that would prove one glass too many and ... Oh, it was endless. They would come all right. Sick today, dead tomorrow, and on Thursday Bellman & Black would open its doors to the bereaved. It was an enterprise that could not fail.

He, William Bellman, had created this great engine. It was his, and tomorrow his staff could be coal to its stoves, water to its wheel, and when the customers came thronging, his machine would start to extract the money from them and disgorge them changed, lighter in the pocket and lighter at heart, as the process took their guineas and replaced them with consolation. He had made it. It was his emporium, Bellman &—

His hands were shaking. He had forgotten something. Never in his life had he been more certain! A feather stir in his abdomen, a turbulence in his chest: he was on the brink of remembering.

Uh-oh. Do you get the feeling that William Bellman's self-satisfaction is a bit premature? You're right. What Bellman doesn't grasp is that he is atoning for his disregard for the lives of others, beginning with his casual childhood killing of the rook. As he enjoys great health, his family sickens and dies. As he rises to enormous success through relentless hard work, he misses out on life. The gift of his beautiful singing voice goes unused. Mr. Black gives Bellman what he wants but takes away what Bellman most needs.

Don't mess with rooks, baby, but if you are a fiction writer here's a shiny lesson to hoard: When characters celebrate themselves, make sure that the celebration is tinged with apprehension.

Fireworks also cast shadows.

Gillian Flynn's *Gone Girl* (2012) is a novel full of dark delights and contains the greatest plot twist in recent memory, maybe ever. Along the way, it also offers a reverse of the "I Am" passage: a passage of "I Am Not."

First, though, a little setup.

Gone Girl is a past-present novel in two halves. The first half is narrated by Nick Dunne, a morally lazy guy who, washed out of New York magazine writing, now co-owns a bar with his sister in dumpy Carthage, Missouri. The second half is retroactively given over to Nick's wife, Amy, the daughter of a pair of child-neglecting children's book authors, whose wildly successful series character, Amazing Amy, was ever-so-ironically named after her.

At the beginning of the novel, Amy goes missing, apparently abducted and possibly murdered. Nick is the prime suspect and evidence against him mounts relentlessly. As a narrator, he proves unreliable, so there's plenty of reason to suspect him. Passages from Amy's candid and warm personal journal, which chronicles their courtship and marriage, are juxtaposed with Nick's distasteful personal revelations. Early on, Amy declares one of her foundational principles, which explains one of the reasons she's so perfect for Nick:

> Nick and I, we sometimes laugh, laugh out loud, at the horrible things women make their husbands do to prove their love. The

pointless tasks, the myriad sacrifices, the endless small surrenders. We call these men the dancing monkeys.

Nick will come home, sweaty and salty and beer-loose from a day at the ballpark, and I'll curl up in his lap, ask him about the game, ask him if his friend Jack had a good time, and he'll say, "Oh, he came down with a case of the dancing monkeys—poor Jennifer was having a 'real stressful week' and really needed him at home."

Or his buddy at work, who can't go out for drinks because his girlfriend really needs him to stop by some bistro where she is having dinner with a friend from out of town. So they can finally meet. And so she can show how obedient her monkey is: He comes when I call, and look how well groomed!

Wear this, don't wear that. Do this chore now and do this chore when you get a chance and by that I mean now. And definitely, definitely, give up the things you love for me, so I will have proof that you love me best. It's the female pissing contest—as we swan around our book clubs and cocktail hours, there are few things women love more than being able to detail the sacrifices our men make for us. A call-and-response, the response being: "Ohhh, that's so sweet."

I am happy not to be in that club. I don't partake, I don't get off on emotional coercion, on forcing Nick to play some happy-hubby role—the shrugging, cheerful, dutiful taking out the trash, honey! role. Every wife's dream man, the counterpoint to every man's fantasy of the sweet, hot, laid-back woman who loves sex and a stiff drink.

I like to think I am confident and secure and mature enough to know Nick loves me without him constantly proving it. I don't need pathetic dancing-money scenarios to repeat to my friends; I am content with letting him be himself.

I don't know why women find that so hard.

Guys, does this sound too good to be true? Doth the lady protest too much? Hoo, baby, watch out. Flynn is playing games with her characters and with us. Big games. Our perceptions are at high risk and if you think you know what's really going on, wait. You don't. Flynn's universe is one in which nothing is as it seems. We know that from Nick's narration and from the plot surprises that Flynn unfolds until the novel's disturbing conclusion.

The passage above, by declaring "I Am Not," paradoxically causes us to wonder, *Well then, who are you?* Flynn dares us to believe whether what we're hearing is true, which, I'm happy to report, it never is. Flynn is playing head games with us. She's also showing us that me-centered narration, to stir us, needs a dose of something that makes us worry, or at least doubt.

Most of all, something that makes us doubt ourselves. Me-centered narration goes beyond simple me-me-me to capture that which makes *me* a topic for discussion, disagreement, and discovery. When the *me* in every scene is a mystery, a moving target, a dynamic force, and a taut trampoline off of which we can bounce, well then, we bounce. When characters show us that they are complex, we feel complex, too. We chew on them, and ourselves, as well.

And isn't that the effect you want?

EMOTIONAL MASTERY 3: ME-CENTERED NARRATION

- Pick any scene in the middle of your novel, one in which your protagonist is the POV character.
- Write an exploratory version of the scene that is about what's happening—not in the plot per se, but about what's happening with "me." What does your protagonist feel about this place, each scene participant, what's happening, and herself?
- How do your protagonist's feelings about any of the above shift in this scene? What has your protagonist overlooked? About what or whom was your protagonist wrong, or dead right?
- What new feeling about the scene's action does your protagonist discover? What new feeling about himself does your protagonist also find?
- Use your protagonist's feelings to mislead the reader about something, or instead to convey the honest truth. Use "I am" to create uneasiness. Use "I am not" to create doubt.

- How much of what you've written in this version of the scene could be folded into your manuscript? Use it.

We feel *me* mostly in what characters need emotionally, which is separate from what they need in order to get through the immediate plot problem. When that need is felt, by us, you can begin to play with it in ways that will twist us this way and that, questioning, keeping us emotionally off balance, which is to say emotionally involved. Just as the outcome of a scene can be in doubt, a character's emotional outcome can also be a source of suspense.

EMOTIONAL SCALE

What was the most emotional day of your life? Most people's answers to that question probably are a lot like your own: days involving birth, death, betrayal, trauma, marriage, divorce, miscarriage, failure, second chance, recovery, a dream achieved, a confession of love, getting a helping hand.

But those are events.

Let's look at the emotions they evoke, for these are strong feelings and the ones you'd like readers to feel as they read your fiction. We're talking about big primary emotions such as fear, rage, passion, glee, ecstasy, triumph, hope, astonishment, grief, humility, joy, or love.

You probably are *not* thinking about mild emotions like apathy, boredom, caring, contentment, doubt, fondness, gloom, melancholy, liking, or satisfaction. Rarely is the aim to evoke moderate feelings. Mostly the goal is to provoke feelings in readers so large and memorable that they're described as experiences.

You might think that to give readers such experiences you need only work with primary emotions. However, there's a problem with that: Big emotions often fall flat on the page. Trying to evoke them through showing can fail to work any better. Tiptoeing down creaky stairs into a dark basement doesn't necessarily instill fear. A dozen roses don't automatically deliver love to our doorsteps. Flying bullets don't cause our hearts to pump.

Listen to genre writers talk and you'd think that their stories are designed to evoke only one gigantic feeling, perhaps dread, terror, joy, or love. While there's nothing wrong with hoping readers will feel those things, mostly they do not. Why? Partly because those feelings are familiar and the scenarios that are supposed to evoke them are often humdrum. If story world is dystopian, for instance, does it make you want to stock guns and hoard food? Does a dead body on page one shatter your sense of security? Of course not.

How could a story possibly provoke such feelings? It can't. It's not real.

And yet we do feel strongly, sometimes, when we're reading fiction. Big feelings like dread, terror, joy, or love can be evoked in readers, but not by force. They are most effectively evoked by trickery. Stage magicians use misdirection to take their audiences by surprise. Emotional craft is similar. Artful fiction surprises readers with their own feelings.

Thus, creating big feelings in readers requires laying a foundation on top of which readers build their own towering experience. What is that foundation? The more precise question is, what triggers readers to dredge up their own emotional experiences? One answer is this: It's the small details (reminders) used to evoke a situation that are preloaded with feeling.

Or just remember this: details. Details have the power of suggestion. Suggestion evokes feelings in readers, drawing them out rather than pounding them with emotional hammer blows.

Stephen King's *Doctor Sleep* (2013) is his sequel to *The Shining* (1977). The little boy from the Overlook Hotel, Dan Torrance, who survived his father's violent possession and breakdown, is now, as an adult in his forties, a drifter and a drunk. He drinks to stave off the torment of his paranormal gift, the shining. Dan lands in a small New Hampshire town, joins AA, and finds work at a hospice, where his gift helps him comfort dying patients and usher them to the other side. We see this gift at work one evening when Dan is called to the bedside of ninety-one-year-old Charlie Hayes:

> "I'm pretty scared," Charlie said. His voice was little more than a whisper. The low, steady moan of the wind outside was louder. "I didn't think I would be, but I am."
>
> "There's nothing to be scared of."
>
> Instead of taking Charlie's pulse—there was really no point— he took one of the old man's hands in his. He saw Charlie's twin sons at four, on swings. He saw Charlie's wife pulling down a shade in the bedroom, wearing nothing but the slip of Belgian lace he'd bought her for their first anniversary; saw how her ponytail swung over one shoulder when she turned to look at him, her face lit in a smile that was all yes. He saw a Farmall tractor with a striped umbrella raised over the seat. He smelled bacon and heard Frank Sinatra singing "Come Fly with Me" from a cracked Motorola radio sitting on a worktable littered with tools. He saw a hubcap full of rain reflecting a red barn. He tasted blueberries and gutted a deer and fished in some distant lake whose surface was dappled by steady autumn rain. He was sixty, dancing with his wife in the American Legion hall. He was thirty, splitting wood. He was five, wearing shorts and pulling a red wagon. Then the pictures blurred together, the way cards do when they're shuffled in the hands of an expert, and the wind was blowing big snow down from the mountains, and in here was the silence and Azzie's solemn watching eyes. At times like this, Dan knew what he was in for. At times like this he regretted none of the pain and sorrow and anger and horror, because they had brought him here to this room while the wind whooped outside. Charlie Hayes had come to the border.

The moment of death. What a heavy thing to capture. Yet what makes it both vivid and bearable in King's passage are the small details of a life well lived. *He saw a hubcap full of rain reflecting a red barn.* King works with visual and sensory images not to describe death but to rapidly chronicle life and thereby this imminent death—*Charlie Hayes had come to the border*—becomes not a dark unknown but a poignant celebration of what was beautiful and light.

By the way, the "Azzie" mentioned in the previous passage is the hospice's cat. King has said that what partly inspired *Doctor Sleep* was a news story about Oscar, a therapy cat in Providence, Rhode Island, who allegedly is able to predict the deaths of terminally ill patients.

EMOTIONAL MASTERY 4:
SMALL DETAILS EQUAL BIG EMOTIONS

- Pick a point in your manuscript in which the predominant feeling is large and primary. If you're unsure, choose the moment in which your protagonist feels the greatest fear.
- What are small signs that indicate something large is happening? What details, hints, indirect clues, or visible effects have you used?
- What repercussions of what's happening can the reader immediately see?
- What does your protagonist or POV character feel that is not immediate? How will she change, do something differently from now on, or see another person, or anything at all, in a way that's forever altered?
- What can your protagonist or POV character say or think that's not obvious, but insightful, unusually compassionate, brutally cutting, or prescient? What can he quip or point out ironically?
- What is a way of looking at what's happening that scales it down to manageable size? In what way is this outrageous event actually unsurprising? How does it illustrate a truth or apply in all cases? In what way is it unique?
- Craft a passage in which you convey not the primary emotion that your protagonist or POV character is feeling but the experience that she is going through. Use details, unusual feelings, non-obvious observations, calm detachment, and wise compassion.

Next, let's look at the opposite end of emotional scale: working with small emotions. The ordinary flow of everyday feelings presents the opposite challenge. Rather than evoke big feelings with small details, you want small emotions to have big impact.

So how is that done?

In life what we feel moment by moment matters greatly to us but little to others. To us, our days are full of high drama, ups, downs, and stomach-plunging swings. Naturally you don't expect others to take your feelings as seriously as you do, yet on the page you're asking readers to do just that: to be rapt and fascinated by your characters' every tiny mood swing.

That won't be the case until you make the emotional minutiae of your characters' lives worth your readers' time. A monotonous pattern of action-reaction will not do that. It's what I call *churning*, or the recycling of feelings that readers have already felt. It's easy stuff to skim. To get readers fully engaged in emotional minutiae requires, again, catching readers by surprise.

When characters struggle with their feelings, readers must referee. They seek to resolve characters' inner conflicts. They render judgments. The same is true when characters feel the unexpected. Readers hold an instant inner debate, one of which they are largely unaware but that nevertheless causes them to assess. *Would I feel like that, too?* That assessment is the effect you are going for.

The heartfelt and playful historical romances of Kate Noble tend to mix cheeky, aristocratic romance with touches of mystery and espionage, locating her in the neighborhood of historical romance stalwarts such as Mary Balogh, Eloisa James, Julia Quinn, Loretta Chase, and Joanna Bourne. The third novel in Noble's Blue Raven series, *The Summer of You* (2010), is the story of Lady Jane Cummings, who appeared in the immediately prior novel in the series.

Lady Jane is a lively, party-loving young duchess who adores the London season but whose father, a duke, is in declining health due to a dementia that would be recognized today as a deepening stage of Alzheimer's disease. When it's determined that the duke's health would benefit from residence in the countryside, Lady Jane must accompany her father to their family's summer estate on Merrymere Lake, where she spent many happy childhood days. Accompanying them are her father's new nurse and her cranky, carousing, perpetual-student brother, Jason. He is even less happy than Jane to be leaving London but nevertheless insists on tending to their father's well-being.

As their party coaches northward, Jane recalls her childhood journeys to Merrymere Lake:

> Or at least, she intended to sulk. To rail against the injustice of being taken out of the cream of society at the height of her popularity, forced on her by a lost old man and dunderheaded young one. But then, over the course of the journey, days spent rambling down familiar roads with two snoring companions, something strange occurred.
>
> It started with the gnarled oak tree, the one that sat a few miles outside of Stafford, on the North Road. The Beast, she had called it as a child. The massive growth that rose from the ground like a boil on the earth, the moss that covered its black hide a faded green, blending the Beast into the grass it sat upon. Its leaves fell like wisps of hair on a bald man's head, and the Beast was so tall and so thick that when Jane was little and of a frightfully macabre mind, she was certain it would eat passersby and force them to live in its knotted innards. But then, Jane's mother, seeing that her daughter cowered whenever they passed the tree, whispered in the child's ear that the tree wasn't about to devour them as they trotted by in the barouche. Nay, the gnarled old tree was in fact the manor house of the Fairy Lord—and instead of holding her breath as they passed, she should wave hello, and the fairies would lift the limbs of the tree, and it would wave back.
>
> …
>
> Every year after, even when she was long past the age of believing in Fairy Lords, she would wave to the Beast, taking a childish delight

in its rumpled visage as it waved back, or didn't, on the whims of the breeze.

...

By the time the carriage of the Duke of Rayne passed the Bridgedown Fell, where if one sat up very tall, they could see the first glimpse of the blue waters of Merrymere, the lake the Cottage was situated upon, Jane was sitting so high in her seat she bumped her head on the window frame of the carriage door.

"Looking at the water?" Jason yawned from his perch aboard Midas. "I thought you weren't excited by going back to Reston."

"I'm not excited," she countered. "But I must have something to do—these two snore too loudly for me to hope for sleep."

Jason harrumphed, but he could not fool his ever-watchful sister. He was sitting suspiciously high in his seat, too.

This journey from London to the Lake District could have been humdrum and flat, and would have been in lesser hands, but Noble uses it to create an emotional passage by enlarging a roadside sight and underplaying the all-too-evident mutual pleasure of an otherwise bickering brother and sister. It's a small moment large in emotion, because the author finds feelings where we're not looking.

EMOTIONAL MASTERY 5:
SMALL EMOTIONS EQUAL LARGE EXPERIENCE

- Choose a small but meaningful moment in your story. From whose POV are you writing this moment? What does he feel about what is happening?
- Discard that. Instead write down a contrasting feeling that your POV character also has. Make the contrast sharp, ironic, forceful, principled, passionate, or in any other way a challenge to the reader's own feelings.
- Considering the moment, what's one implication of what's happening? What will your POV character have to do differently

now? What must your POV character do that is hard, against the grain, or in any other way unwelcome?

- What's one way in which this character must question herself at this moment? Go beyond self-doubt. Render a self-judgment. Is this character condemned? How? Is this character exonerated? How?
- At this moment are we in heaven or hell? Why? What is wonderful? What is unbearable? How does your POV character reconcile to this moment and what it means? What's the outrage? What's the wisdom?
- Craft a passage in which the big meaning of this small moment is processed by your POV character, a processing that's unique to this character and contrary to your reader's own feelings—maybe even to yours.

The trick, then, is to give readers emotional content that is not just easy to swallow but, rather, a feast to savor. Any small emotional moment can thus achieve an effect larger than it might otherwise have.

STIRRING HIGHER EMOTIONS

Who are your personal heroes? Is there a historical figure that inspires you? Isn't that how you'd like your readers to feel about your characters?

Optimism, vision, dedication, high achievement, and leadership are not everyday qualities. Compassion, empathy, and understanding—even for an enemy—are rare. Gandhi, Martin Luther King Jr., and Mother Teresa are not common. However, we're not talking about life; we're talking about fiction. Why not create characters that inspire us to a high degree?

It's disappointing that so many characters I meet in manuscripts are ordinary in their makeup. They aren't in the great classics, nor need they be in your current novel. Who your characters are, how they behave, what they believe, how they think, what they do, and the ways in which they feel are in your control. Why create characters who only raise shrugs?

In 1771, Thomas Jefferson wrote to his friend Thomas Skipwith to recommend that Skipwith include works of fiction in his library. He said this was because "everything is useful which contributes to fix us in the principles and practice of virtue. When any ... act of charity or of gratitude, for instance, is presented either to our sight or imagination, we are deeply impressed with its beauty and feel a strong desire in ourselves of doing charitable and grateful acts also." In other words, virtuous acts by fictional characters inspire us to be virtuous, too.

More recently Dr. Jonathan Haidt and others have scientifically demonstrated that fiction can have an effect called *moral elevation*, which affirms that reading about good people causes us to be better ourselves. We make better choices when characters inspire us to do so. To that I would add that we also remember good acts more than bad ones. Betrayal and cruelty shock for a moment but fade from our minds. Sacrifice, heroism, selflessness, and grace endure in our hearts and become that to which we aspire. We remember. We emulate.

When we are moved and inspired by the actions of characters, what we feel are *higher emotions*. They are the timeless virtues extolled in every religion and recommended by every great thinker. Higher emotions make us ponder. They make us change. They make us better people. They also cause readers to rate those novels more highly, which isn't bad either.

When reason prevails over impulse, when disgust is replaced by insight, when an act of generosity is undeserved, when love is given where rejection seems certain, when someone sticks up for another, when help is unasked for, when apology is humbly made and forgiveness unexpectedly given, when doors are opened in welcome, when truths are spoken and the origins of conflict laid bare, such acts stir in readers the swelling of the chest and opening of the heart.

Taking a stand for what's right is without question one of the greatest emotional tools available. R.J. Ellory's international best-seller and multiple-award-nominated *A Quiet Belief in Angels* (2007) is initially set in 1939 in the small town of Augusta Falls in Georgia. Its protagonist is twelve-year-old Joseph Vaughn, who forms a protective group called The Guardians after several girls are murdered in the area. However, he's only a kid and the forces of fear and prejudice around him are strong.

Suspicion falls on a local farmer, Gunther Kruger. World War II has begun and suspicion of German-Americans is running high. Kruger becomes the target of hate crimes, and when xenophobic speculation erupts at a birthday party, the responsibility falls upon the town sheriff, Haynes Dearing, to stand up for Kruger's constitutional rights:

> Haynes Daring raised his hand. "Enough already. I'm still the law, and I'm layin' it down. This here's a birthday party for Clement Yates, and that's all it's gonna be. We ain't rattlin' our cans about nothin' like that this evenin'. We got Leonard Stowell and Garrick McRae here, both of them lost little 'uns." Dearing raised his eyes and then nodded at each man in turn. "Different news for a different day, agreed?"
>
> "Didn't come here to say nothin' about nothin'," McRae said, "but while that pie is on the table I'll cut a slice … I agree with Clement, birthday or no birthday, it ain't no American."
>
> "Last one was a Jewish girl," Frank Turow remarked.
>
> "Ain't important what kind of girl she was," Lowell Shaner said. "Fact of the matter was that she was someone's daughter, and I was out there on the line after Garrick's daughter was murdered … I was out there watching grown men who'd never even seen her before, and I saw those men darn near break down in tears. They went

　　　THE EMOTIONAL CRAFT OF FICTION

out there 'cause they wanted to help ... and I'll tell you something right here and now Sheriff—"

Dearing leaned forward, his head set between his hunched shoulders like some kind of fighting dog. "And what're you gonna tell me, Lowell Shaner?"

For a heartbeat Shaner looked doubtful, but he glanced at Garrick McRae, could see the grim line of the man's tense jaw, the flinty hardness of his eyes, and the dense substance of that expression seemed to give him the resolve he needed.

"That if something ain't done sharpish—"

"Then you good ol' boys are gonna get yourself a lynching party all soaked up with spirits, pour yourselves into the back of a flatbed, and go haring off down to St. George or Moniac and hang yo'selves some poor dumb defenseless nigra. Tell me I'm wrong and I'll give ya each a dollar."

An awkward silence joined the party.

"Nigras is Americans," Clement Yates said quietly.

"Well, right enough," Dearing said. "I'm sorry, I missed the drift of this thing. What you're talking about is finding some foreign child killer ... like an Irisher perhaps, or maybe one of them Swedes that came through here on the way to the logging camps ... or hell, what about a German? We got plenty of Germans here."

...

"We're not gonna have any trouble here in August Falls," [Dearing] said quietly. He leaned forward once more and laid his hands flat on the table, palms down. "We're not gonna have any trouble here, and it ain't gonna be because I said so, it's gonna be because what we got here is some straight-thinking, sensible citizens, all of you more than capable of stringing some words together into a short sentence, all of you wise in the ways of the world, all of you suffering a little with the heat, the bad crops, perhaps ... but none of you suffering from the hot-headed band foolish malady called witch-hunting. We agreed on this point?"

There was a moment's hesitation as each man scanned the faces of the collective remainder.

"Are we agreed on this point?" Dearing asked a second time.

A murmur of consent traversed from left to right.

Well, okay! The force of right and reason is a force to be reckoned with, one that cannot help but rouse folks, whether poor farmers or jaded readers. Even morally corrupt characters can rise at times to produce a similar effect.

John Ajvide Lindqvist's reinvention of the vampire novel, *Let the Right One In* (2004), is the story of a bullied twelve-year-old boy, Oskar, living in a working-class suburb of Stockholm with his mother. Oskar becomes fascinated by the odd girl living next door, Eli, a child vampire who helps Oskar with his adversaries.

Eli's adult human cohabitant, the tormented pederast and child abuser Håkan, obtains blood for her. Lindquist's novel is about as dark as fiction gets, dealing with issues from social isolation to pedophilia to self-mutilation to murder. Despite that, the novel also portrays great acts of self-sacrifice, one of the largest of which (and it's a big one) is carried out by Håkan for Eli. Why would an irredeemable character do such a thing?

Lindqvist needed to prepare his readers for that and so created an early scene to foreshadow Håkan's later sacrifice. In this earlier scene, Håkan, in a public bathroom with ten thousand kronor bills in his pocket, solicits child sex. (Caution: a strong stomach is needed for the following; skip it if you are squeamish or have moral objections to portraying vile acts.)

> The outer door opened. [Håkan] held his breath. Something in him hoped it was a policeman. A large male policeman who would kick open the door to the booth and beat him up with the baton before arresting him.
>
> Low voices, soft steps, a light knock on the door.
>
> "Yes?"

...

A boy about eleven or twelve stood there. Blond hair, heart-shaped face. Thick lips and large, blue eyes devoid of expression. A red puffy jacket that was a little too big for him. Right behind him was the older boy in the leather coat. He held up five fingers.

"Five hundred."

...

He looked at the boy he had bought. Hired. Was he on drugs? Probably. The look in his eyes was far away, unfocused. The boy stood pressed up against the door half a meter away. He was so short that Håkan didn't need to tilt his head to look into his eyes.

"Hello."

The boy didn't answer, just shook his head, pointed to his groin, and made a gesture with his finger: unzip your pants. He obeyed. The boy sighed, made a new gesture: take out your penis.

...

He narrowed his eyes, tried to imagine the boy's gestures so they more closely resembled his beloved [Eli]. It didn't work so well. His beloved was beautiful. This boy, who now bent down and pushed his head toward his groin, was not.

His mouth.

There was something wrong with the boy's mouth. He put his hand to the boy's forehead before he reached his goal.

"Your mouth?"

The boy shook his head and pushed on his hand so he could continue his work. But now Håkan couldn't. He had heard about this kind of thing.

He put his thumb against the boy's upper lip and pulled up. The boy had no teeth. Someone had knocked or pulled them out in order to make him more fit for his work.

...

Not like this. Never like this.

Something came into his line of vision. An outstretched hand. Five fingers. Five hundred.

He took the pack of bills out of his pocket and handed it to the boy. The boy took off the rubber band, ran his pointed finger across the ten pieces of paper, replaced the rubber band and held the packet aloft.

"Why?"

"Because … your mouth. Maybe you can … get new teeth."

The boy smiled a little. Not a wide grin, but the corners of his mouth pulled up. Perhaps he was only smiling at Håkan's folly. The boy thought for a moment, then took a thousand kronor note from the packet and put it in his outer pocket. Put the rest in an inner pocket. Håkan nodded.

The boy unlocked the door, hesitated. Then he turned to Håkan, stroked his cheek.

"Sank you."

I warned you. As ugly as that situation is, there is something beautiful in Håkan's gesture. He is low, no question. Earlier in the novel he drained the blood from a boy who was hung upside down like a pig. Even so, he is shamed by his desires. He can sacrifice. Ten thousand kronor may be little enough, but it's enough to give us the idea that even the worst example of humanity can still have a heart.

Perhaps it's this spirit that led *Let the Right One In* to become an international bestseller and to inspire two film adaptations (in Swedish and English) and a West End stage version.

Moral stands and struggles have emotional power, and it's a rare story that could not generate such moments and achieve that power. All characters can rise above their own selfishness, for a moment, to become gracious, insightful, generous, or self-sacrificing.

We all shine at times, so why not your characters, too?

THE EMOTIONAL CRAFT OF FICTION

EMOTIONAL MASTERY 6: GOOD DEEDS

- Think about your protagonist. What is one good thing your protagonist finds exceptionally hard to do?
- Work backward to make that virtuous act even more difficult. Later on, perhaps following a catharsis, find a way for your protagonist to do, at last, that good deed.
- Build a secondary character that is selfish, self-absorbed, self-pitying, put upon, wounded, or treated unjustly. What is the selfless act this character would never be expected or called upon to do? Make it happen.
- Which character has a low opinion of another? Reverse it later in the novel, showing that the judgmental character has hidden compassion and insight.
- Which character has a justified grudge against another? Build the reasons for it, then enact forgiveness.
- Which character is miserly? Choose a moment of celebration or ceremony for that character to give an unexpected gift.
- In what way can your protagonist self-sacrifice, giving up something (or someone) dear?

MORAL STAKES

We tend to think of Western culture as a postmodern wasteland: amoral, materialistic, self-aggrandizing, and dogmatic. The truth is that we all yearn for a better world, one filled with compassion, respect, justice, opportunity, equality, and freedom. You can see this in politics. Conservatives and liberals both want a better world, even though they seek different roads to achieve it. You can see this in beliefs. Both followers of faith and rational scientists seek purity and truth. You can see this in cultures. People of all backgrounds value family, community, and shared customs. Human beings are good.

Given the universal hope for what is high and right, it's surprising to me that characters in fiction so often have their eyes fixed on the ground. Their focus is on what is immediately in front of them, as if the current plot complication is all that matters. I am not against giving plot problems greater personal meaning; indeed, I teach a method of raising *personal stakes*, which develops just that. Equally important, though, are a story's *moral stakes*.

What happens when a protagonist doesn't act virtuously? What is lost? Unfortunately, what's lost is readers' respect for the protagonist. That's crucial because whether or not your protagonist is a good person matters to readers. It's the first thing they look for and a prerequisite for their involvement in your story. Antiheroes and dark protagonists would seem to be an exception, but not really. When they work it's a trick. Dark characters we care about secretly signal something to us. However bad they may seem, underneath they are good.

It's important to signal to readers that a character is good, and you should do so early in the book. One obvious method is to *save the cat*, the screenwriters' technique of showing small demonstrations of worthiness. Fiction employs a greater range of such signals, many based in self-awareness. Even miserable characters who demonstrate a glimmer of wry humor, a sharp eye, or a strong voice can win us over, at least for a little while, since we trust that someone who is observant, alert, and self-aware has the potential to become good.

That said, nothing builds reader involvement more surely than a character whose moral struggle pervades the tale. When readers hope, beg, and plead with you to let a character turn toward the light, you have readers where you want them. A character who is good is good; a character whom we *want* to be good is even better.

Not just any dark, miserable protagonist will trigger that feeling in us, though. To hold out hope for a protagonist, we must first feel that there is something to hope for. Struggle is the key. Trying to be good is at least trying. Other characters can also stand in for us, having unearned faith in a character whom everyone else in the story has little reason to trust.

The arc of moral change isn't complete when change itself arrives. An insight gained, an understanding reached, the end of inner conflict, or the arrival of inner peace are fine, but there is one more step: proof. When a person has changed, we can see it. A selfish person turns selfless. An inward person looks outward. For authors, it's a kind of giving back. When inner peace has arrived, it's time for a transformed character to put good into the world.

The literary thrillers of Chris Bohjalian are enviable. They pull off what every author would like to do: make a suspenseful story without resorting to the FBI, nuclear terrorism, serial killers, or other familiar devices. They are about regular people whose stories are nevertheless thrilling page-turners.

Bohjalian's *The Double Bind* (2007) goes one better by employing a literary conceit: The story is set in a slightly alternate reality in which the West Egg and tragic events of Fitzgerald's *The Great Gatsby* are presumed to have actually happened.

In our own times, Laurel Estabrook, a social worker at a Vermont homeless shelter, curates a collection of highly artistic photographs left in a box by a mentally ill and now deceased resident, Bobbie Crocker. Among the shots of midcentury celebrities, jazz artists, and Greenwich Village in its heyday are pictures of a place Laurel recognizes: West Egg (where she grew up) and the Gatsby Mansion, whose ugly romantic history still overshadows her hometown.

However, there is an even more disturbing photograph in Bobbie Crocker's collection. It's a recent picture of a country road in a nearby Vermont town, a female cyclist in the distance. Laurel recognizes the cyclist as herself and the road as the one she cycled down the day she was raped, mutilated, and nearly abducted. The photograph was taken shortly before the attack.

Unhinged by this discovery, Laurel becomes convinced that Bobbie Crocker and his photographs hold the key to why she was attacked, and that there is a connection back to West Egg and the Buchanan family. Indeed there is a connection, but Crocker's family secrets prove a fresh, potent danger to the already damaged Laurel.

Laurel's regular life goes on with her older boyfriend (newspaper editor David Fuller), her fast-living theology student roommate (Talia), and their well-meaning and smitten rooming-house neighbor (Whit), whose attempts to invite Laurel on a cycling date are comically clueless. It's Whit who provides a lesson in moral transformation. One summer night he, Laurel, Talia, and a group of college friends go dancing. On the way home they come upon a reeking homeless transient, unkempt, unwashed, covered with sores, and whispering to himself. The group moves to pass by, but ...

> Laurel went right to him. She squatted before him and got his attention. Asked him his name and told him hers. She certainly didn't pull him completely from his own planet back to theirs, but while Whit and Eva had stood unmoving and mute, fearful, Laurel was taking his hand in hers—and Whit understood clearly that taking the soiled hand of a transient was an act both of mercy and of bravery—and leading him to his feet. Laurel told them that they should go on ahead, but they didn't. They went with her as she escorted the man to the shelter. There were beds left because it was summer and the homeless can endure a lot longer outside, and with the night manager's help she got him showered and fed, and then she convinced him to sleep inside that night. It took her about an hour to get him settled. The fellow didn't talk to the rest of them. He really didn't say a whole lot to Laurel. But he stopped his murmuring and his eyes no longer darted like the orbs in a pinball machine. They locked on to Laurel's, and it was clear he felt safe around her. Whatever conspiracies were after him, whatever delusions had led him to the street, momentarily they were checked.

When Laurel rejoined Eva and Whit, she apologized for costing them an hour of sleep, and the three of them resumed their walk up the hill. Whit was shaken both by the stink and the utter hopelessness of the fellow Laurel had brought in from the street and by his first view of the inside of the shelter. But after four years there, plus her time as a volunteer, Laurel, he saw, had thought nothing of it. And he, in turn, was left not merely smitten. He was awed.

Whit's not the only one who's impressed. Acts of courage and generosity have the power to change us, even when they're made up. Bohjalian's purpose in including this scene might be to explain why Whit is smitten with Laurel or to show that the damaged Laurel has compassion for the also damaged homeless, or to reassure us that even though Laurel is obsessed with Bobbie Crocker's photographs, she remains normal and anchored in her work.

Any of those would be good enough reasons to include this scene in his novel, but Bohjalian also uses it to crack open our hearts a bit more. A demonstration of goodness and care will do that. Laurel's generosity is inspiring, especially considering that she herself is a survivor. More than that, naïve Whit is transformed by her act of courage and loves her more, so that we can, too.

(Incidentally, if you should read *The Double Bind*, hang on for one of the most astonishing trick endings in recent fiction. It's a doozy.)

Moral struggle and moral choices can have an elevating effect, too. Harper Lee's late-discovered novel *Go Set a Watchman* (2015) raised controversy over the author's mental fitness and the circumstances of its discovery and publication, but mostly it created anxiety due to the hallowed reverence the public has for her only other novel *To Kill a Mockingbird* (1960), a treasured coming-of-age novel about racism in the South.

The controversy intensified when early reviews came in. In *Go Set a Watchman*, a now grown-up Scout returns to her hometown, Maycomb, from New York City, where she has been living, to decide whether she can truly love her father's young law partner, Henry (Hank) Clinton. In the earlier novel, *To Kill a Mockingbird*, Scout's father, Atticus Finch, was an icon of rectitude, justice, and color blindness. In *Go Set a Watchman*, an older Atticus tolerates racist views.

What was lost amid the hand wringing was that *Go Set a Watchman* is nevertheless a fine—if quieter—novel with a similar theme. In the novel, grown-up Scout, who is once again known by her proper name, Jean Louise, faces a crisis when her Aunt Alexandra alerts her that Atticus is attending a Maycomb County Citizens' Council Meeting, a type of organization well known as a cover for discrimination. Jean Louise then attends the meeting in time to hear that day's featured member speak:

> She had never seen or heard of Mr. O'Hanlon in her life. From the gist of his introductory remarks, however, Mr. O'Hanlon made plain to her who he was—he was an ordinary, God-fearing man just like any ordinary man, who had quit his job to devote his full time to the preservation of segregation. *Well, some people have strange fancies,* she thought.
>
> Mr. O'Hanlon had light-brown hair, blue eyes, a mulish face, a shocking necktie, and no coat. He unbuttoned his collar, untied his tie, blinked his eyes, ran his hand through his hair, and got down to business:
>
> Mr. O'Hanlon was born and bred in the South, went to school there, married a southern lady, lived all his life there, and his main interest today was to uphold the Southern Way of Life and no niggers and no Supreme Court was going to tell him or anybody else what to do ... a race as hammer-headed as ... essential inferiority ... kinky woolly head ... still in the trees ... greasy smelly ... marry your daughters ... mongrelize the race ... mongrelize ... mongrelize ... save the South ... Black Monday ... lower than cockroaches ... God made the races ... nobody knows why but He intended

for 'em to stay apart … if He hadn't He'd've made us all one color
… back to Africa …

[Jean Louise then remembers her father conducting a defense for
Tom Robinson, a black man wrongly accused of rape, yet here he
is today.]

Jean Louise's hand slipped. She removed it from the balcony railing and looked at it. It was dripping wet. A wet place on the railing
mirrored thin light coming through the upper windows. She stared
at her father sitting to the right of Mr. O'Hanlon, and she did not
believe what she saw. She stared at Henry [Hank] sitting to the left
of Mr. O'Hanlon, and she did not believe what she saw …
    … but they were sitting all over the courtroom. Men of sub-
stance and character, responsible men, good men. Men of all vari-
eties and reputations … it seemed that the only man in the county
not present was Uncle Jack. Uncle Jack—she was supposed to go
see him sometime. When?
    She knew little of the affairs of men, but she knew that her fa-
ther's presence at the table with a man who spewed filth from his
mouth—did that make it less filthy? No. It condoned.
    She felt sick. Her stomach shut, she began to tremble.
    Hank.

Jean Louise's disgust is the moral heart of *Go Set a Watchman*,
showing that Harper Lee no more supported segregation in her
trunk novel than she did in her famous debut. Following her
discovery, Jean Louise must reconcile with, or reject, men whom
she loves. Morally speaking we might want her to walk away and
wash her hands of Maycomb and its men, but life isn't that simple.

Go Set a Watchman gives us a more nuanced and realistic view
of the South in the years immediately before the Civil Rights movement, so even if that disturbs our reverence for the Atticus Finch of
To Kill a Mockingbird, is that not to Harper Lee's credit? Whether or
not you agree, it's impossible to be neutral about either the novel or

its topic. Harper Lee's writing makes us emotional no matter what, which is the effect we want.

EMOTIONAL MASTERY 7: MORAL STAKES

- Identify a higher emotion you'd like your readers to feel: self-control, courage, perseverance, truthfulness, fairness, respect, generosity, forgiveness, service, sacrifice, discernment, integrity, humility, readiness, or wisdom.
- Choose a character whose nature is, or whom you can make, the opposite of this quality. Who most needs to learn this lesson, see a truth, adopt this virtue, and change?
- Prepare the groundwork for change. Give this character every reason to be the opposite of what he will become. Reinforce that that opposite way of being works and is the right way to be. Find a way to show that at the start.
- Create three events that both build the necessity of change and necessary reasons to resist it. These events are the anticipation phase.
- Finally, create the event that will bring home to your character the better way of being. How can this character show us her better self? This is the moment when you will stir higher emotion in your readers.

The emotional world of the story is mysterious, but not to you. For you, it's a plot of its own, a puzzle begging a solution, a journey that needs to be taken, and a landscape that serves your story purposes. Focus on the emotional world of your characters and you will not only make a better tale, but you will build a better world for us all.

CHAPTER FOUR

EMOTIONS, MEANING, *and* ARC

I'd like to get to know you. I mean, really *know* you. Would you do me a favor? Please fill in this questionnaire:

Date of Birth:

Hometown:

Elementary School:

High School:

College/Major:

Occupation:

Date of Marriage:

Other Marriages:

Current Residence:

Religious Affiliation (if applicable):

Awards/Honors:

Hobbies/Interests:

Thank you! Now we're like old friends, right? Wait, we're not? What did I miss? Oh yeah, all the important stuff. What I didn't ask about are the events that have shaped you into the person that you are today. I know nothing of the meaningful life events that do not appear on your resume. To truly know you I'd have to ask questions like these:

What's the first thing you remember making you truly happy?

When and how did you discover that life isn't fair?

Who first broke your heart?

What accomplishment proved to you that you can do anything?

When did you decide you had to grow up?

What did you learn about yourself in your twenties?

How did that change in your thirties?

What's been your biggest sacrifice?

What was the most romantic night of your life?

Whom have you loved beyond reason?

What disgusts you?

What food can't you resist?

If you ran the world, what's the first thing you would change?

What's the biggest thing left on your bucket list?

How did you find—or reject—God?

What shapes us and gives our lives meaning are not the things that happen to us, but their significance. Life lessons, revelations, changes, and growing convictions are what we think of when we ponder who we are.

As we experience the events of our days, we process them and make them personal. We document our lives not just with visual images, but with narration that explains what those images mean. We aren't just resumes, the dry sum total of our accomplishments and anniversaries. We are stories.

Plot happens outside but story happens inside. Readers won't get the true story, though, unless you put it on the page—both the big meaning in small events and the overlooked implications of large plot turns.

When you illuminate the meaning of everything, you can do anything. You can deliver dry facts and make them matter. You can tie together a narrative that spans decades or lifetimes. You can make poetry out of doing the dishes. Anything you put on the page becomes charged with electricity because it's telling the story that your plot doesn't. It's telling the universal story of human growth and change.

What do we mean when we say "meaning"? For our purposes it's not one thing, a single gem of wisdom. It's the stream of insight, understanding, realization, and acceptance that one continually gains from personal experience, and that adds up to the subjective reality called *me*. The *me* in *me*aning is aimed primarily at seeing the significance of our experiences not for others, but for ourselves. We are philosophers of I.

Take dry facts. Almost every story requires that you explain some things to your readers. Scientific, historical, occupational, or local knowledge is needed for the story to make sense. This stuff can sit on the page like a lump. When it does, it's called *info dump*. Or it can feel lively, engaging, and important. That happens when that information means something to a point of view character and you put that down in words.

M.R. Carey's science fictional take on zombies, *The Girl with All the Gifts* (2014), concerns ten-year-old Melanie, who, as we meet her, is locked in an underground cell. On weekdays, she is strapped into a wheelchair and rolled to a classroom with other children who are also strapped down. On weekends, they are given caustic showers and bowls of grubs to eat. One teacher, Helen Justineau, is sympathetic and treats the children like human beings. The head guard, Sgt. Ed Parks, treats them like highly dangerous animals. The head of the place, Dr. Caroline Caldwell, treats them like experimental subjects, which indeed they are. Once in a while, Dr. Caldwell kills and dissects one of them.

On the day Melanie is to be dissected, the military base that hosts the experiment, Hotel Echo, is attacked by a pack of feral, flesh-eating remnants of the human race, informally referred to as *hungries*. Melanie escapes with Helen Justineau, Dr. Caldwell, and Sgt. Parks. Making their way across a devastated Britain, they eventually come upon an abandoned mobile laboratory. In an emotional midpoint (see chapter five), Melanie has discovered that she is a hungry monster, but one who retains rational thought (she can learn) and who can, to some degree, resist the need for human flesh. Melanie still has questions, though. Now free, and perhaps feral, she tricks Dr. Caldwell into the mobile laboratory to demand answers.

Dr. Caldwell is not without attachment to Melanie, her prize subject, a highly intelligent hungry whose biology may hold the key to a cure for the epidemic that has wasted Britain, caused by a fungus known as *Ophiocordyceps unilateralis*. (Hungries eventually decompose and become tree-like organisms.) Dr. Caldwell, however, is dying of an altogether different condition, a blood infection. Her time is limited. She is happy to explain her discoveries to Melanie and does so in a sequence that blends science and sentiment:

> "What do you want from me?" [Caldwell] asks. It's clear from Melanie's agitated manner that she wants something, has something on her mind.
>
> "The truth," Melanie says.
>
> "About what?"
>
> "About everything. About me, and the other children. And why we're different."
>
> [Caldwell begins a scientific explanation of environmental triggers to sporing bodies, and of brain structures.]
>
> But [Caldwell] is at war with herself. Part of her wants to guard the secret, to give away no more than she's asked, to force Melanie to dive deep for every pearl. The other part is desperate to share. Caldwell longs for an auditorium of geniuses, sages both living and dead. She gets a child who is neither, or both. But the world is winding down, and you take what you're given.
>
> "The hungries," she says, "including you, are infected with a fungus named Ophiocordyceps." She assumes no prior knowledge, because there's no telling what Melanie has understood, or failed to understand, from those notes. So she begins by describing the family of hot-wiring parasites—organisms that fool the host's nervous system for forged neurotransmitters, hijacking the host's living brain and making it do what the parasite needs it to do.
>
> Melanie's questions are infrequent, but right on topic. She's a smart kid. Of course she is.
>
> [Caldwell goes on to explain why Melanie is different, having been born with the infection, rather than becoming infected, and how the fungus interacts differently with the brains of second

generation hungries like Melanie. Caldwell gives Melanie her notes and instructions on where to take them.]

When it becomes harder for Caldwell to talk, Melanie comes closer and sits at her feet. The scalpel is still clutched in her hand, but she doesn't bully or threaten now. She just listens. And Caldwell is full of gratitude, because she knows what this lethargy that's flooding her means.

The septicaemia is entering its final phase. She won't live to write her findings down, to astonish the remaining scientific minds of humanity's doomed rearguard with the spectacle of her clear-sightedness and their idiocy. It's just Melanie. Melanie is the messenger sent by providence in her last hour to carry her trophies home.

Caldwell's explanation of the operation of *Ophiocordyceps unilateralis,* its etiology and evolution, could be pretty soporific stuff, but Carey knows that the meaning of this information is greater than its importance to the plot. Its greatest significance is to Caldwell herself, a meaning made more poignant because at the end of her life the only person to whom she can impart her findings is Melanie, the child she intended to kill.

Dry information is only dry when it doesn't mean anything to anyone. What gives information emotional effect is not the facts that it conveys, but the personal significance it holds for someone who understands it.

Novels that span long periods of time have trouble holding together. To the author a whole life is fascinating but to readers it can be just long. What ties together decades' worth of events and makes them one story? Nothing, actually, except the constant of change itself.

No reader will find every phase of a life equally interesting. Events cannot accomplish that, but a ceaseless quest can. Even when life grows routine and its days lack drama, the important questions remain: *What do I want? Have I found it yet? How do things seem different to me now?*

THE EMOTIONAL CRAFT OF FICTION

The mysterious and pseudonymous Italian novelist Elena Ferrante, whose books were described by *The New York Times* as "feminist potboilers," is best known for her Neapolitan Novels, a four-book series about two bright girls who grow up in Naples but whose adult paths diverge even as they remain friends.

Four volumes make for a pretty long story, especially the story of one friendship, yet the series feels both epic and intimate. How does Ferrante pull that off? How does she unify so many pages, stages of life, and periods of time so that they all seem like one tightly woven story?

The third in the sequence, *Those Who Leave and Those Who Stay* (2014), picks up the friends later in life. The one who left Naples, Elena, has established herself as a novelist. Her friend Lina remains in their home city, divorced and working in a factory. The novel's opening finds Elena again in Naples visiting Lina.

While on a walk they come across the dead body of another childhood friend who collapsed in a flowerbed next to a church. Following this unsettling episode, Elena contemplates the city, which has both changed and hasn't:

> The fine winter day gave things a serene aspect. The old neighborhood, unlike us, had remained the same. The low gray houses endured, the courtyard of our games, the dark mouths of the tunnel, and the violence. But the landscape around it had changed. The greenish stretch of the ponds was no longer there, the old canning factory had vanished. In their places was the gleam of glass skyscrapers, once signs of a radiant future that no one had ever believed in. I had registered the changes, all of them, over the years, at times with curiosity, more often carelessly. As a child I had imagined that, beyond the neighborhood, Naples was full of marvels. The skyscraper at the central station, for example, had made a great impression, decades earlier, as it rose, story by story, the skeleton of a building that seemed to us extremely tall, beside the ambitious railroad station. How surprised I was when I passed through the

> Piazza Garibaldi: look how high it is, I said to Lina, to Carmen, to Pasquale, to Ada, to Antonio, to all the companions of those days, as we made our way to the sea, to the edges of the wealthy neighborhoods. At the top, I thought, live the angels, and surely they delight in the whole city. To climb up there, to ascend—how I would have liked that. It was our skyscraper, even if it was outside the neighborhood, a thing that we saw growing day by day. But the work had stopped. When I came back from Pisa, the station skyscraper no longer seemed the symbol of a community that was reviving but, rather, another nest of inefficiency.

Ferrante is too skilled a novelist to write directly about her characters' inner states. Instead she writes around them using analogy, leading us by implication to inescapable points of clarity.

In this passage about Naples, narrated by Elena, what is she really telling us about? Naples? Of course not. She's really talking about herself, her friendship with Lina, the passage of time, and how things both change and don't. Even more so, Elena is saying that what once was new and exciting can stall and become corrupt. What once was a friendship they regarded with pride has become like a place they no longer recognize or want: a sentiment we see played out in the now prickly relationship between the two women.

On an even deeper level, though, Ferrante is unifying her long story by asking in this passage, as she does so often throughout the four volumes, *Who am I right now? What has become of me? How did I get here? How do I see things differently? What did I want and have I found it yet?*

What Elena wants in Ferrante's sequence is a friend—a lifelong, solid, unchanging rock—who can be her anchoring point in the tempest of life. But circumstances change, people change, and relationships change, too. It's a hard lesson but a great story, one that hangs together over many volumes because it is unified by one need, the need for friendship, and the recurring questions that we all ask ourselves about our own lives.

Perhaps the greatest challenge in writing fiction is making ordinary domestic tasks matter enough to read. Have you ever followed a character through a day and thought, *Do we really need to see all of this?* Do you sometimes skim stuff and wish authors or editors had deleted it?

Other authors, though, can crawl through a day and make every moment matter. Their characters comment, ponder, question, and turn over everything that happens to them as if every second of life is a diamond and everything said or heard has facets that demand examination.

Personally, I find the extreme intimacy of contemporary narration sometimes wearisome, but sales figures show that readers value this intimacy. That extreme intimacy speaks to readers and that, in turn, is because those authors have found that everyday events have something to say. There is poetry in doing the dishes if the metaphor is freshly made, a crux, a revelation, or a turning point.

Could anything be more ordinary than using toilet paper? Viet Thanh Nguyen's *The Sympathizer* (2015), winner of the Pulitzer Prize, is the story of an unnamed Vietnamese immigrant, a spy, who recounts his experience as a communist sympathizer in a long, forced confession and emigrates to America after the fall of Saigon in 1975.

How does such a man view the world? At one early point in his experience, the sympathizer becomes a consultant on a propaganda film. He travels to a location shoot in the Philippines, a location that is meant to substitute for Vietnam. A realistic set version of a Vietnamese village has been created by the production designer, Harry:

> Harry showed me the main set the next morning, a complete reproduction of a Central Highlands hamlet down to the outhouse

mounted on a platform above a fishpond. A stack of banana leaves and some old newsprint constituted the toilet paper. Peering through the round porthole of the toilet seat, we could see directly into the deceptively calm waters of the fishpond, which, Harry proudly pointed out, was stocked with a variety of whiskered catfish closely related to the ones of the Mekong Delta. Really ingenious, he said. He had a Minnesotan's admiration for resourcefulness in the face of hardship, bred by generations of people one very bad winter away from starvation and cannibalism.

I had sat on exactly such a splintery toilet seat throughout my childhood, and remembered very well the catfish jockeying for the best seat at the dining table when I assumed the position. The sight of an authentic outhouse stirred neither any sentimental feelings in me nor any admiration for my people's environmental consciousness. I preferred a flush toilet with a smooth porcelain seat and a newspaper on my lap as reading matter, not between my legs. The paper with which the West wiped itself was softer than the paper with which the rest of the world blew its nose, although this was only a metaphorical comparison. The rest of the world would have been stunned at the luxurious idea of even using paper to blow one's nose. Paper was for writing things like this confession, not for mopping up excretions.

I have never given much thought to the meaning of toilet paper, but for someone whom paper of any sort is a luxury, its significance is something else. *Paper was for writings things like this confession.* Nguyen's metaphor grows elaborate in this passage, but its meaning hits home. Paper is precious. Toilet paper is an unimaginable luxury to many. Is it also a luxury to confess? Or, perhaps, is his confession worth no more than toilet paper? Nguyen's narrator is a spy, a traitor; he's slippery, elusive, unreliable, and yet a man who passionately longs to tell us about himself, to get us to understand even the tiny details of his experience.

THE EMOTIONAL CRAFT OF FICTION

Meaning lifts the mundane to new levels, and with it our feelings. When a character is struck by the meaning of everyday things, we cannot help being struck by that character.

EMOTIONAL MASTERY 8:
THE MEANING OF EVERYTHING

- Choose any small thing that happens somewhere in the middle of your manuscript. When you find it, write down your answers to the following questions: This small event is symbolic, but symbolic of what? What does it mean to your POV character personally? What meaning might anyone see if they bothered to look? How is your POV character's understanding of himself changed in this moment, even in a small way?
- Choose some dry information that must be imparted for your story to make sense. Who has this knowledge? How does that character see these facts as no one else does? What standard of judgment is used? What is good, bad, worrisome, reassuring, or in some other way revealing about these facts? What does your character love or hate about what these facts are saying? What would she change about this information if possible? What would he change about himself?
- If the span of your story is long and it covers one character's experience, stop at four points along the way and at each ask: Right now, what is your protagonist seeking for herself? What does your protagonist need to find? Why is that newly important now? Is this character closer to, or farther away from, what he needs? What is the measure of progress? What is encouraging? What says give up? Has this character yet become who she needs to become? Is that a problem, or is that okay for now?
- Turn those notes into a paragraph or passage to add at this point in your manuscript. Don't be afraid of slowing the pace. When you deepen the meaning of things, no one will complain.

As human beings we seek self-knowledge, wholeness, happiness, and love. We yearn to explain the inexplicable; to justify our existence;

and to understand who we are, why we're here, and what we're supposed to do.

It's a quest that never ends. We may have dens with trophies on the mantels, but when we tell the stories of our lives, we relate the meaning of things that happened and describe how we grew. Our stories are as unique as snowflakes. They do not happen in the predictable patterns that writers call plot templates. They happen all the time, at odd moments, and in ways that only we can see. So it is with your characters. Their stories are happening always, and it is up to you to reveal how.

You may think you are telling your characters' stories, but actually you are telling us ours. Unearth the significance of any moment for a character and you will reveal its universal value.

CONNECTING THE INNER AND OUTER JOURNEY

I spend a lot of time in airports. Wait around as much as I do and you begin to admire airport design. Think the TWA Terminal at JFK, Terminal B at SJC, the International Terminal at SFO, the passenger arrival canopy at PDX, or the mountain range roof of DEN. Gorgeous. High. Open. Airy. Look toward the sky and you're already in flight.

Look a bit closer, though, and you may also feel afraid. The structural components that support these architectural confections do not inspire confidence. What, really, is holding these buildings up?

Not much.

Now, shop-welded and field-bolted shear connections I understand. These are the trustworthy old plates and flanges that connect steel columns and beams, transferring the bearing load and resisting rotation and bending "moment." They're rigid. Strong. Think Empire State Building and you've got the idea.

THE EMOTIONAL CRAFT OF FICTION

Contemporary design, however, values visible structural elements. Architects want the skeletons of airports to look lightweight. They also want ease of assembly and tolerance for slightly variable element lengths. Face it: Clunky old shear connections are not cool. Airport architecture shouldn't look like it's from the era of lunch pails and union lines, right? It should look contemporary.

Enter the pin connection. A pin connection is a fastener between two structural steel elements, which in airports are often tubes. Imagine an elbow joint. In building terms that means a lapped-type connection involving a U-shaped clevis through which a "pin" (a bolt) passes. It is this little pin that holds two structural pieces together.

It's the pin that worries me, especially when it supports the building's entire bearing load as in a base connection. Stick with me here. Think about it. The whole weight of the airport is resting on the architectural equivalent of the bolt and nut, like one that you keep in a glass jar on your basement workbench. I mean, seriously? The entire weight of a roof is resting on a little bolt?

Those must be strong bolts. And, of course, they are. They have to be. I don't really need to worry. A pin connection is as reliable a way to join steel as is the old-fashioned flange. Maybe more so. The airport roof will stay up. I can enjoy my latte and laptop with ease of mind. The airport is securely fastened together.

What, you ask, does this have to do with writing fiction? The columns and beams of your novel are your protagonist's twin journeys: outer and inner. The outer element, your plot, holds up the novel's structure, like columns hold up a skyscraper. What lends a novel a feeling of depth, perspective, and movement across space, though, are its crosswise beams: your protagonist's inner journey. To be both lightweight and strong, a novel needs both of those things working together.

But what fastens these two elements? How do the inner and outer journeys connect so that they become an architectural wonder? Plot events are what happen. Inner moments give those events meaning. Together they both shelter and lead the reader somewhere new. That new place, ultimately, is up to the sky.

The term *character arc* is well known in the fiction writing game. Every novelist believes that he understands what it means, and most feel they have mastered its use. Some employ different terms like *growth, inner journey,* or *transformative arc,* but they all mean the same thing: the change or changes that a character goes through over a novel's length. Characters start as one kind of person but become another.

Why, then, do I often feel that the inner journey is short, simplistic, or absent in manuscripts? It's often because arc is less a journey than a jump. Many times it's an event at the end that enacts a single change, reform, or realization. It's more an add-on bonus than an ever-present quest and ongoing struggle.

Most character arcs are malnourished. It's not easy to write inner struggle. It takes skill and courage to keep it on the page without making it a drag. Who wants to read a dull and repetitive wallowing in the worst parts of oneself? No wonder authors avoid it. However, the architecture of a novel is not made up of plot alone. Beams may hold your story up in the air, but they won't move it anywhere emotionally.

The sense of movement in a story comes mostly from inside. It's a tidal pull, an emotional tug. It says not just that things are going to change but that people are going to change. It's ongoing. In life, change isn't annual. It's daily. We change constantly, maybe every hour. We are forever evolving in our understanding of self, others, and the world. We are awake, alert, and alive. We ponder. We learn. Life is what we do, certainly, but even more it's what we take away from it.

It's odd, then, that on the page so many protagonists go through events of high drama and seem to change very little. What do they think about of what's happening? What do they feel? How do they feel about *themselves?* You may believe it's better to leave that to the reader, but remember that readers don't create—they react. Readers compare themselves to characters but there must be something to compare *to.*

Most authors can say how their protagonists need to change. Most can name their characters' struggles. The greater difficulty is making those things an integral part of the story—if not the story itself. So much focus goes into plot mechanics. Setting, theme, and voice get a lot of attention, too. They're easier to pin down than the characters' messy interior lives. Yet as much as any other element in a novel, the inner mess needs to be shaped into story. Tools that form the formless are needed.

But really, what is so difficult about that? As in our real lives, the raw material of the inner journey is ever present. You only need recognize it, make space for it on the page, and treat it like it matters.

To fasten the inner and outer journey, you only need to start with one element: either a plot event or a step in the inner journey. In the first case, go inside your protagonist to pinpoint what an outer event means. In the second case, stop at any inner moment and make something outward happen, something that symbolizes what's going on inside. Outer events lead inward. Inward struggles turn outward.

Are you struggling with this concept? Try imagining this: Your protagonist has a superpower. It's the ability to project her inner state onto the world. What she feels inside makes things happen.

L.A. Meyer's young adult adventure story *Bloody Jack* (2002) was inspired by nineteenth-century songs about young girls dressed up as boys and going to sea. The songs concerned girls following boys, but Meyer wondered what it would be like for a girl to get on board a British warship just to eat regularly. So, he relocated his story to the London slums in the late 1700s and created an orphan named Mary. Born into a middle-class family, Mary is cast out on the street when her family dies of disease. She joins a street gang that lives under a bridge, led by a fair-minded and cheerful lad named Charlie. When Charlie is murdered, though, Mary realizes her life cannot go on this way.

Because she can read, Mary wins a berth on the *HMS Dolphin* as the schoolteacher's assistant. In his novel's opening, though, Meyer tackles the task of convincing his readers that this is something that a girl of the time would do. After Mary takes Charlie's clothes, she chops her hair short to disguise and protect herself, and soon is hailed by a gentleman to hold his horse while he dines in a tavern.

For her trouble, he gives her a penny.

> When he gets on his horse and leaves, I heads into the same tavern and for me penny I gets a bowl of stew and a bit of bread, which is something wonderful. I licks the bowl clean, tucks the bread in me vest for later, wipes me mouth on me sleeve, and heads out.
>
> It's easier bein' a boy, I reflects.
>
> It's easier bein' a boy, 'cause nobody bothers with you. Like, I couldn't have gone into that tavern yesterday as a girl 'cause they would have shouted, "Get out of here, you filthy girl," while they didn't say anything when I went in as a filthy boy. My filthy penny was as good as anyone else's.
>
> It's easier bein' a boy, 'cause no one remarks upon me bein' alone. Lots of boys are alone but girls never are. The girls gets scooped up into beggin' and stealin' gangs, or workhouses, or worse. True, on my journey south I was eyed by some gentlemen of the street who thought as they would look better in me vest than me, but a flash of me shiv put some caution in 'em and that was that.
>
> It's easier bein' a boy, 'cause when someone needs somethin' done like holdin' a horse, they'll always pick a boy 'cause they think the dumbest boy will be better at it than the brightest girl, which is stupid, but there you are.
>
> It's easier bein' a boy, 'cause I don't have to look out for no one but me. I'm feelin' a great sense of freedom, like a weight's been

THE EMOTIONAL CRAFT OF FICTION

lifted from me shoulders, as I'm dartin' me way down to the docks. I'm feelin' a little ashamed for feelin' so light, too, what with Charlie dead and me leavin' the others and all, but that's the way it is.

I slips between two loose boards into a stable that's all closed up for the night, and I burrows in the warm and sweet smellin' hay.

I decide my name will be Jack.

Mary/Jack's journey takes her from girl to boy—and then back again. Does the plot demand this, or is her voyage at sea a consequence of her decision to switch genders? It's hard to say, but there's no doubt that the two necessities—outer survival and inner need—come together in this moment.

Even in a simply written, swashbuckling children's adventure tale, the inner and outer journeys join. As a result, we can easily buy into both Mary's gender switch and the highly entertaining naval adventure upon which she embarks.

EMOTIONAL MASTERY 9:
CONNECTING THE INNER AND OUTER JOURNEY

• Pick any plot event, large or small. What does it mean to your protagonist? What does it stir inside? What worry, hope, question, or wonder? What does it feel like to *feel* this feeling? Create a metaphor for it. Make notes. Write it up in a paragraph.

Or ...

• Pick any emotionally significant moment in your story, a time when your protagonist feels himself changing. Shut off inner monologue. Find a way for your protagonist to show or speak the unfolding inner change in a way that we can't miss. What is your character compelled to do? Do it.

What you're doing, simply put, is using thoughts and feelings as fasteners. What happens means something, and when meaning arrives, it makes something happen. Steel joins steel. The lightest pin holds it together. Fasten together enough components, inner and outer, and you have architecture, a story that conveys both what happens and how a human being is reaching for the sky.

TENSION VERSUS ENERGY

What is more comfortable for you to write, feelings or action? It's an important question. The answer predicts what we'll mostly find on your pages, but also what we mostly won't. While it's fine to fill pages with what is natural and easy for you, it's also critical to get comfortable writing what isn't natural and easy.

Human beings can be divided into two broad psychological categories: those who store tension and those who store energy. Those things may sound the same but they're not. People who store tension turn inward. Those who store energy turn outward. The first group ponders, reflects, thinks, and feels. The latter group acts. One set of people likes to deal with life over a cup of tea with a splash of conversation. The other set prefers to go for a run or smack a ball with a stick.

If that sounds like a gender dichotomy, you may be right. Psychologist Paul Rosenfels, in his work identifying *polarity* in people's makeup, agrees. He does not assert that one way of being is better than the other; rather, he observes that the orientation of feeling-centric and action-oriented people comes with advantages and disadvantages. Each group has their best selves and their worst selves.

There is no judgment in polarities. There is only the recognition that a person is more naturally one type over the other. That's important for fiction writers to know, too, and especially important as you focus on constructing the journey of a character's change and fastening it to that character's journey through the plot.

When what a character does follows a shift inside, that action feels authentic. It can work the other way, too. Tension building up inside seeks release, a burst of steam from an inner pressure valve.

This principle matters because in many manuscripts characters act as they do only because of plot imperatives. That's okay, but that feels inauthentic and has low emotional effect.

Polarity swings, on the other hand, create a hidden inner trigger to action. They make it possible for characters to shift into action, or out of it, when there's no outwardly logical reason to do so. Polarity swings make plot developments happen when there is no plot. Things feel as if they are moving forward even if the story's circumstances aren't. Polarity swings provide pace of a different sort: emotional pace.

Put plainly, it's the swings *between* polarities that cause characters and their stories to grip us as if they are real.

Characters dwell in a state of being. At any point in a story their selves can be defined. However, a state of being by itself is static; changing states are dynamic, and what is story if not change? As I have written elsewhere, what makes any given scene dynamic is not changing story circumstances, but changing characters.

So what kind of polarity swings are we talking about? Ones like these: self-awareness turning into self-confidence; goodness hardening into righteousness; the feeling of safety transforming into the feeling of freedom; observing the world transforming into taking responsibility for it. Crafting polarity swings at times means shifting characters into high gear. As obvious as that sounds, I often watch writers in workshops freeze when it's time for their characters to stick their necks out, do something we can't miss, say things that cannot be taken back, or make an inconvenient mess.

Characters are the most interesting when they're inconvenient. Making them behave that way can be uncomfortable, of course. Writing fiction with emotional effect requires feeling easy with uneasiness.

There is also the opposite issue: downshifting from action into reflection, backing off from outward conflict and delving into inner turmoil. Some writers find that equally difficult. Still, novels need not just plot pace but emotional pace. They need to shift emotional tempo and change emotional key.

Getting practical, let's look at polarity swings in two directions: first from tension to energy, then from energy to tension. Notice how outer action and inner life play off each other. They're not enemies, as we'll see.

Alex Gordon's debut *Gideon* (2015) is about Lauren Reardon, who, upon her father's death, learns that Matthew Mullin was not his name and that he is from a town that she has never heard of—and one that does not seem to exist: Gideon, Illinois. Among his papers is a frail volume called *The Book of Endor*, printed in 1871, "In this year of the Great Fire." Lauren becomes determined to learn the truth about her father, and Gideon.

Gideon, we already know from early backstory chapters, was a town of witches. Its tragic history begins in 1836 when the misguided town elders elect to burn a powerful rogue witch, named Nicholas Blaine, at the stake. Mistakes are made, warnings go unheeded, but Nicholas Blaine is immolated nonetheless. But he does not die. Said to be the son of the devil himself, Blaine returns in 1871 to destroy Gideon. First, he tempts mistress Eliza Mullin, a scene witnessed by Joe Petrie—a boy at the time of Blaine's burning who is now a veteran of the Civil War.

As Gideon begins to burn to the ground, Joe Petrie points a Colt revolver at Nicholas Blaine. He knows he should kill him, but how can you kill someone who's already dead?

> Eliza Mullin stopped pacing and turned to Petrie. "Get out, Joe." Another sigil, the very air rippling with the movement of her hand. "Go. Now."
>
> "I can't leave you with him." Petrie tried again to aim the Colt at Blaine, but his hand shook like palsy, too weak to pull the trigger. "I can't."

"But you will." Blaine wheeled, coat swirling like a mage's gown. "Because you can smell the smoke and hear the flames roaring into the upper floors. The attic. The roof." He took a step toward Petrie. Another. "Leave the lady behind, Joseph, as you left so many men behind on the battlefield. Men you called friends until you learned the coward's truth, that friends are nothing more than bodies to hide behind."

"Don't listen to him." Eliza Mullin's voice rose above the growing din. "He'll fog your mind and turn your fears against you." Her voice softened, a mother's comforting murmur. "It's all right to be afraid, Joe."

Petrie snorted. "You're not."

"Shows what you know."

[The fire intensifies.]

A sob rose in Petrie's throat. He looked to Eliza Mullin, who now stood still, hands folded like a mourning angel.

"Go, Joe." Not a request this time. An order.

"Yes, go, Joe!" Blaine clapped his hands, the sound muffled by his gloves. "Run, run, run—"

Another crash sounded. It drove Petrie like a whip—he hurtled down the narrow hallway as the ceiling rained fire and Nick Blaine's laughter rang in his ears. As he reached the rear door, he looked back in time to see the flames shoot out of the parlor like the exhalation of a dragon. In the space of a heartbeat, the hallway became an inferno.

Petrie fled into the night, past the other burning houses, through the ring of fire that had been Gideon's town square. He ran past old men, women and children, ignored the shouts and cries for help, the calls for missing loved ones.

Run, Joseph Petrie. It's what you do best.

From frozen in fear to running in retreat and the recognition that *I am a coward*: Joe Petrie's inner tension turns to energy, but with it comes an emotional price. There's plenty of action in this fiery scene, but an even more terrible burning inside. The shift up from one mode to the other, tension to energy, and back again, makes this a scene not only about fire, but about the scorching of a very real, if flawed, human being.

Natasha Pulley's *The Watchmaker of Filigree Street* (2015) is set in London in 1883 and concerns a clerk in the Home Office telegraphy department, Thaniel Steepleton, whose small and dreary life changes when a unique pocket watch suddenly appears in his room. This watch, as we learn, may be revealing events yet to occur. It's protecting him. That's useful because it's an era when the Fenians, Irish revolutionaries and forerunners of the IRA, are planting bombs in London.

A telegraph decoded by Thaniel alerts him that the Home Office itself is to become a bombing target. The day, and then the hour, of the anticipated bombing has everyone on edge:

> As nine o'clock edged around, the office began to slow. The clip of Morse was more spaced as the telegraphists listened for an explosion. In the larger office across the corridor, the typists lost their rhythm and lowered their voices. Thaniel saw Park's knuckles whiten over his telegraph key. He leaned across and took it from him gently, and got up to cross the corridor. The telegraph room was windowless, but the typists' office had huge windows overlooking Whitehall Street. The others followed him. They found the typists standing too, going to the same window. It was open now and letting in the smell of ozone. Thunder growled around the city steeples, quietly, as though it knew that hundreds of men were trying to listen.
>
> Nine chimes tolled out from Parliament and the city remained its ordinary self, unlit by slashes or smoke. Rain tapped on the window panes. The clerks exchanged glances, but nobody moved. Thaniel took out the watch. A minute past, two minutes, and still nothing. Ten. Then a gust of laughter came from across the street. The clerks from the Foreign Office were already on their way home. They were sharing umbrellas.

The senior clerk rang his bell.

"Well done, everyone! Early shift is over, late begins in two minutes. Clear out, and if you see an Irishman on your way home, give him a good kick from the Home Office."

There was a cheer, and he took his first deep breath for months. He hadn't been aware of breathing shallowly. It had happened gradually; someone had put a penny on his chest every hour since November, and now the weight of thousands of pennies had lifted at once.

The energy at the beginning of the passage is present in the signs of stress in the Home Office clerks as they await a blast. The relaxing of that tension occurs in Thaniel, who becomes aware that he has been breathing shallowly for months and that now the "weight of thousands of pennies" has lifted. If you've ever relaxed a white-knuckle grip on the armrest of a seat in an airplane leaving a patch of turbulence, then you know how Thaniel feels. The energy you felt was the fear of death. The tension that replaced it was the feeling that you'd been foolish to doubt that you would live.

EMOTIONAL MASTERY 10:
SHIFTING FROM TENSION TO ENERGY

Write down your answers to the following:

- Choose a moment when your protagonist sees or hears something unjust. A braver person would get involved. How?
- Your protagonist is good at something. A more commanding person would turn that into a show of strength. How?
- Your protagonist is helpful. A bolder person would be reckless. In what way?
- Your protagonist has insight into someone else. A more compassionate person would show that person kindness. How?
- Your protagonist is peaceful. A true leader would maintain peace by exerting power. In terms of your story, how?
- Your protagonist is a misfit, doesn't conform, and feels like an outsider. A more independent person would be a nonconformist, even break the law. When?

- There is something or someone who makes your protagonist impatient. A more headstrong person would be wholly intolerant. How would we see that?
- There is someone to whom your protagonist feels attached. A more engaged person would get deeply involved. How?
- Pick a time when your protagonist is withdrawn or distant. A more passionate person would completely detach and not care. How would we recognize that?
- Your protagonist is self-focused, even self-important. A stronger (weaker?) personality would be simply vain. What, in particular, is your protagonist self-focused on?
- Your protagonist has a logical way of looking at a problem. A more intuitive person would not think about it but instead do something unexpected and ingenious. What?
- Your protagonist is attracted to someone. A more uninhibited person would lean in for the kiss or send an unmistakable kiss-me signal. What?
- Your protagonist can do magic. A greater mage can work miracles. What's the biggest?
- Your protagonist is wise. A truly transcendent human being brings about the impossible. What in your story is impossible?

Do your answers suggest ways to make your protagonist more active, vibrant, surprising, and memorable? If so, use them.

In life, our moods swing. We contradict ourselves. We act out of character. We act out. Why then is it so hard to allow characters to do the same? We all swing between the polarities inside us. We second-guess ourselves, judge ourselves, have insight into ourselves, gain from hindsight, and make intuitive leaps. We also blunder ahead, ignore warnings, fail to think before speaking, dive in, reverse course, dance in the end zone, throw up our hands, throw punches when we shouldn't, and walk away when we should hold firm and take a stand.

Polarity swings are steps in the emotional plot, so why not pace your novel accordingly? If you do, readers will feel an inner heartbeat marching them ahead, a pulse that's independent of the visible story events that distract our eyes.

EMOTIONAL MASTERY 11:
SHIFTING FROM ENERGY TO TENSION

Write down your answers to the following and elaborate each:

- Your protagonist has a way of life. What is her view of life?
- Your protagonist has a strong sense of purpose but also a strong unfulfilled need. What is that need, and how does your protagonist regard it?
- Choose a time when your protagonist shows courage. At the same time, in what does he also gain faith?
- Find a point at which your protagonist is in control. What does she come to understand—or not?
- In one realm your protagonist is assertive. In what other realm does your protagonist yield, and why?
- Your protagonist relishes adventure. When does that come into conflict with romantic love? How does your protagonist measure the two against each other?
- When does your protagonist show the strongest leadership? What must he teach?
- Your protagonist is good. What is something that she finds beautiful and why?
- Your protagonist is audacious, but about what is he perfectly sincere?
- Your protagonist rebels. How does she realize that she has also committed heresy?
- Your protagonist is a loner or finds himself alone. How does this also seem to your protagonist a form of poverty?
- Your protagonist enacts justice. How does she realize that she must also show mercy?

If your answers to any of the above give you ways to open up the inner life of your protagonist in interesting ways, use them.

CHAPTER FIVE

The EMOTIONAL PLOT

Most fiction writers have a pretty good grasp of plot. They work on it, worry about it, and use templates as varied as snowflakes and the hero's journey to develop it. Scene checklists help them keep things moving. Microtension keeps readers turning every page. Get plot down and your novel will have a firm foundation, right? True enough, and yet even airtight plots can fail to keep us emotionally engaged. Why is that?

Let's discuss.

Many authors motivate their characters with external circumstances. *I must do* this, *because if I don't,* that *will happen.* The stakes in such stories are also external. Things need to come out right or, gosh, life will be terrible for everyone. There's nothing wrong with what I call public stakes; they just don't have automatic emotional effect.

Personal stakes are the more reliable way to make a story matter to readers. Personal stakes are why protagonists must act for themselves. It's the drive that comes from inner need and yearning. It's what would propel a protagonist toward change, even if the events of the novel weren't happening.

Plot excites our interest. It pulls us along with its urgent questions, tension, and, we hope, uncertainty about what will happen next. What holds our hearts in suspense, though, is the tension inherent in where self is going next. That excites our emotions. That excitement can be generated by inner need but more precisely by restlessness, resistance, searching, slow surrender, a sense of being alien, or knowing that one is incomplete. The cause can be as specific as a secret or as broad as existential angst. It's invisible yet palpable.

We all yearn. Things happen to us. We cope, solve problems, suffer setbacks, get somewhere, and pursue our dreams. What, though, actually drives us to do those things? Something inside that has little to do with our challenges and goals. It's a need to relieve inner anxiety, prove something, love and be loved, rage at what's unfair, fit in, stand out, or find what will make us happy.

Do plot events kick off a story or does the story (the one inside, I mean) kick off a novel's events? You can look at this as a chicken-or-egg question, but I think it's more useful to embrace the duality of fiction: outer journey and inner journey working together. They amplify each other.

Middle moments, the dark hour of loneliness and identity crisis, are similarly twofold. It takes a plot catastrophe to sink a character, but the most terrifying chasm is the one seen in the mirror. A catharsis, likewise, is acting out, but that only works when something has been held in. It also releases new powers, which arrive not as a boon from the gods, but as a discovery of one's own previously hidden potential. The middles of novels happen as much on the inside as on the surface.

The journey toward wholeness is a mysterious one, with turns in the road coming at any time and in any number of ways. Indeed, in our lives it is the unanticipated discoveries about ourselves that have the most lasting effect. Along the way, there are obvious mentors, such as parents, teachers, and coaches, but also unexpected ones like ghosts, barn swallows, and beggars. The struggle with self is the substance of our own stories. Insights are its daily developments and its happy endings are something that can't be measured in material terms: the end of struggle and the arrival of peace.

To reconcile to oneself, to be happy, is a primary human need. To transcend oneself, though, is a divine attainment. The former is enough to make a story good. The latter is what makes a story *great*. The search for peace is satisfied when a protagonist feels happy, but it isn't finished until a hero is also happy with the world. What's inward radiates outward again. In a real sense, the purpose of stories is not only to change characters, but also to point the way to a change in us all.

How can you accomplish that? When you think about it, the effect that a novel has on us is not produced by who is in it, where it's set, or what happens there. It's produced by how we feel about those things. It's a series of emotional kisses and blows. Mile-a-minute thrillers can leave us cold and heavy-breathing romances can make us roll our eyes. On the other hand, stories that have no precedent, little action, a quiet voice, and a mundane setting can move, shake, and change us.

Plot without emotional power is empty, but it gains that power when plot events are treated as emotional opportunities. So let's, for now, forget about plotting your novel and look at how to shape it into emotion-generating moments. What follows are the methods

THE EMOTIONAL CRAFT OF FICTION

of building emotional plot. This is not the plot that keeps us turning pages; it's the plot that keeps us turning things over in our hearts, measuring the protagonist against ourselves and discovering what matters, and why.

EMOTIONAL OPENINGS

A great deal has been written about openings. Without question they are important. The opening is the first impression. It creates a story promise. It poses questions that need answers. It pulls us into a story world. It sets events in motion, or at least establishes a mood. We meet a voice, sense the story's purpose, get a hint of its meaning, and generally settle into the flow of something already moving.

In short, we are intrigued. Indeed most advice about openings is geared toward enhancing our curiosity. Independent editor Ray Rhamey's first-page checklist is an excellent yardstick for measuring what makes openings interesting. Noah Lukeman's book *The First Five Pages* is a detailed discussion of what makes openings uninteresting, listing in order of importance the reasons why agents dismiss manuscripts and suggesting solutions. The term "narrative hook" has its own Wikipedia entry. It's pretty hard not to get the idea. The first job of an opening is to intrigue.

Or is it? Since openings are so important, let's spend extra time on them.

Research psychology has some interesting things to tell us about why people seek out entertainment and what gets them involved in it. To us, it's obvious why we need stories and why they appeal. To scientists, it's a great puzzle. Why do people get caught up in events that they know cannot be real? What causes people to feel strongly about fictional characters, argue with them, and even reimagine their outcomes?

Yes, scientists really study this stuff. Seeking out a story to experience demonstrates what scientists call *intentional motivation*.

The processing of a story then involves *sensory memory, working memory,* an *episode buffer,* and finally retention in *long-term memory.* While we speak of hunts and campfires, scientists posit *Attribution Theory, Cognitive-Experiential Self Theory, Cultivation Theory, Social Judgment Theory,* and *Thematic Compensation Hypothesis.* Still with me here?

Being caught up in a story excites scientists to terms like *transportation, anticipatory empathy,* and *counterfactual thinking.* Most significant of all is the reason that readers sink into a story at all: *Disposition Theory.*

I'll save you some time. Here's what all that means ...

First of all, some support for intrigue: To entertain, a story must present novelty, challenge, and/or aesthetic value. A story causes what psychologists call *cognitive evaluation* in readers, which in plain English means having to think, guess, question, and compare. Making us think as we read not only makes a story intriguing, but medically speaking it's necessary for our well-being and mental health.

Put simply, to be healthy we have to experience wonder. It's one of the reasons that reading stories feels necessary. It actually is.

Having to think about a story also increases its chances of making it into long-term memory. That's because the more we cause readers to chew on a story, the longer it churns in working memory, and that in turn keeps the passageway into long-term memory open. Force the reader to figure something out. Take the reader aback. Make the reader decide something. Insight, new information, surprise, and/or moral challenges all excite cognition, or what we call pondering.

But hold on. Intrigue is not all that it takes. Readers need something else to sink into a story.

It's this: Readers want an emotional experience. They want to feel something, not about the story but about themselves. While reading, they want a sense of play. They want to anticipate, guess, think, and judge, true, but they also want to emerge from a story feeling competent, like they have been through something.

Most important, they want to feel as if they've connected with a story's characters, living their fictional experience. Creating that "as if" experience takes more than just walking readers through the plot. Readers retain a story only when they have felt it. Feeling can be provoked by plot developments, obviously, but only to a limited extent. Plot twists and turns mostly cause simple surprise.

That's fine as far as it goes, but a deeper bond is generated by something that readers feel for a story's characters, not simple plot points. That happens initially when readers are able to make immediate, positive moral judgments about characters, which is to say when they see something good in them. Psychologists call this *affective disposition*. We call it liking, or more precisely admiring. It's why novelists make their characters appealing. It's why screenwriters save the cat. But that is only the start. A given day does not become deeply emotional at sunrise; it's the rest of the day that makes it so.

This need to feel for characters explains some puzzling things about fiction. For instance, why is it that in order to keep us going, thriller writers must keep their characters in jeopardy and constantly running, whereas romance writers can churn a single-note plot conflict (*I love you/I resist you*) over and over again, with no discernable plot movement, and nevertheless create an absorbing and dynamic story experience?

Thrillers and romances are at opposite ends of a spectrum: pure intrigue versus pure emotional involvement. However, the combination that is most effective in producing reader involvement is equal doses of both. When plot hook and emotional hook happen together, they work together. Intrigue opens readers to emotional connection; emotional connection magnifies those elements in a story world that cause readers to marvel, question, and wonder. The best openings, then, create both intrigue and involvement.

So how do we make that one-two punch happen? Plot hooks don't worry me. Most manuscripts have those. What many do not have are emotional hooks, meaning a simple reason to care about a character—which is to say apprehend something good about them—as soon as we meet. Readers almost instantaneously pick up cues and form their judgments, so it is literally true that we must accomplish this bonding on page one. Put more simply, readers know right away whether a character is worth their time.

What, then, do we perceive as a "good" character? The answer varies by reader, but generally characters who are the most universally appealing are models for what we might call heart values. Compassion, insight, a commitment to justice, family, love, steadfastness, sacrifice, selflessness, and other virtues hook readers faster and harder than survival, striving for success, desiring fame, alienation, or aloneness.

Genre writers may find this focus on the warm and fuzzy side of characters counterintuitive. Science fiction and fantasy writers, for instance, know that their readers love to quickly immerse in worlds with different rules. Thriller writers know that establishing a mood of menace is job number one. Heck, no matter what kind of fiction you write, everyone knows that you've got to hit your protagonist right away with a question or a need, if not an outright problem. How are you supposed to go all warm and fuzzy while you're slamming your protagonist in the face with a baseball bat?

Well, that is exactly the kind of two-handed skill that great openings pull off. Consider the opening of Suzanne Collins's *The Hunger Games* (2008). On the face of it, it's a rule breaker: a waking-up-in-the-morning opening:

> When I wake up, the other side of the bed is cold. My fingers stretch out, seeking Prim's warmth but finding only the rough canvas cover of the mattress. She must have had bad dreams and climbed in with our mother. Of course, she did. This is the day of the reaping.

Whoa, wait, what? *The reaping?* What kind of Shirley Jackson nightmare is this? That right there is the intrigue. The emotional engagement is what happens before that bombshell. What does Katniss Everdeen do as soon as she wakes? Whom does she reach for and care about? Her sister, Prim. Right away we know that Katniss has a heart.

The opening of Harper Lee's *To Kill a Mockingbird* (1960) is also a rule breaker, a low-tension backstory passage that dwells on an insignificant detail. Or does it?

> When he was nearly thirteen, my brother Jem got his arm badly broken at the elbow. When it healed, and Jem's fears of never being able to play football were assuaged, he was seldom self-conscious about his injury. His left arm was somewhat shorter than his right; when he stood or walked, the back of his hand was at right angles to his body, his thumb parallel to his thigh. He couldn't have cared less, so long as he could pass and punt.
>
> When enough years had gone by to enable us to look back on them, we sometimes discussed the events leading up to his accident. I maintain that the Ewells started it all, but Jem, who was four years my senior, said it started long before that. He said it began the summer Dill came to us, when Dill first gave us the idea of making Boo Radley come out.

Excuse me? *Boo Radley?* You had me at the character named Dill, but Boo? Okay, I'm hooked. Or at any rate, hooked enough to keep me going for a spell. Harper Lee has taken care of intrigue.

But what about the emotional hook? This is a little tougher to identify, but I would say that once again it's family. The narrator, Scout, cares enough about her brother to be concerned whether his broken arm will affect his self-esteem. (Not at all, she reassures us.) She also gives due respect to his opinion on the origin of "the events leading up to his accident." Scout is looking back from a distance of some years, but because she remains close to her brother, we know that it's safe to immediately feel close to her. She cares, we care. It's safe to lend our hearts to Scout.

Family is a durable way to create warmth in a main character, but of course it's not the only way. Check your shelves, and you'll see that qualities of strength, humor, humanity, and goodness find a way to glimmer just a little in any novel that gets its double hooks into you. So how can you get those hooks into your own readers?

EMOTIONAL MASTERY 12: THE EMOTIONAL HOOK

- As your novel opens, find something warm and human that your main character cares about. If your story is exotic, choose something we would care about in the here and now. If your story has an ordinary setting, find something about which your protagonist is passionate. Open with this feeling.
- Now find in your opening situation something different, odd, curious, puzzling, weird, contradictory, a paradox, or hard to explain. Highlight it. Don't pile on more or explain too much too soon. Let the mystery posed or question raised work on your reader for a bit. There's tension in the unknown.

It's funny that something that sounds so simple is lacking in so many manuscripts. I think that's because intrigue gets all the attention. Involvement is just as important, though, and the best beginning is one that delivers both.

WHY READERS REALLY FALL IN LOVE WITH PROTAGONISTS

People fall in love for all kinds of reasons. They fall for people that you or I wouldn't consider. My idea of a partner is probably not yours. What appeals to me probably doesn't appeal to you. The notion of universal appeal is wrong, and in writing fiction it's impossible to create a protagonist who has that type of appeal. It can't be done.

What, then, are you supposed to do in crafting your protagonist? The first principle to accept is that your main character is not going to be magnetic for everyone. That's not going to happen. On the other hand, you can increase your protagonist's appeal without bleaching out the qualities that make your protagonist distinct and magnetic for you.

In other words, while there's no such thing as a character who is universally appealing, there is such a thing as character qualities that draw us in. Shining qualities appeal the most, but they're not the only ones that are attractive. It's not all about saving the cat.

In life, initial attraction is based on superficial qualities like appearance. That's applicable in making movies, but less useful in fiction. Novelists must bond readers to characters with something else, something about who those characters are. Remember, though, the qualities that make us fall in love: others who reflect, understand, and accept who *we* are. We bond with such people in part not because they're other, but because they're like us.

Sameness would seem to lead us to the timeless principle of creating "sympathy," which in a literary sense means creating a character whose life and circumstances are like ours. An opening that involves the kitchen sink, a flat tire, or changing diapers should be a sure bet for bonding readers to protagonists then, right? Well, no. Of course it's not. Humdrum, everyday life is recognizable but not radioactive. Paradoxically, though, we can bond with characters completely unlike ourselves.

For example, consider how I relate to a typical Gen X or Millennial heroine. I shouldn't. They are completely unlike me. You know the type. Gen X and Millennial heroines have quick wits, but also a sense of helplessness. They are sharply observant but do not command their own destiny. They have complaints and ironic voices.

They feel apart, outside, unnoticed, victimized, and powerless. They don't relate to the grown-up world run by men. In movies, Kristen Stewart and Jennifer Lawrence play these characters.

Gen X and Millennial heroines reflect readers' experience of a world in which parents divorce or are absent, government is a joke, and profit, not principles, rule the world. Guys, meanwhile, are only reliable if they are sensitive-strong-suffering Robert Pattinson types. Gen X and Millennial heroines discover their power, of course, and ultimately take ownership of their lives and destiny. Their narrative tone may be wry but their narrative role is inescapably heroic.

In theory, I shouldn't relate to these heroines who appeal so enormously to young women readers. Clearly, these heroines and their readers are not me, Mr. White Privileged Baby Boomer. However, I love Katniss Everdeen, Bella Swan, and other sad-ironic heroines.

Wait, hold on, aren't Bella and Katniss very different from each other? You might be right about that, but look at their narrative tone and worldviews. Katniss may kick some Panem ass and Bella may only sulk around the Olympic Peninsula and kiss a vampire, but they're both underdogs who are initially powerless, and women surviving in a man's world. So how can I possibly relate to them?

I relate to them for two reasons. Although they are quite unlike me, they are like me in two ways: They have heart and they yearn. They both feel deeply. They both want things, and we feel the ache of that yearning before we even know what they are yearning for.

Let's compare our introductions to Katniss Everdeen and Bella Swan. These are two very popular young adult protagonists, but their authors' approaches and styles are quite different. First, a review of the opening of *The Hunger Games*, mentioned a few pages ago:

> When I wake up, the other side of the bed is cold. My fingers stretch out, seeking Prim's warmth but finding only the rough canvas cover of the mattress. She must have had bad dreams and climbed in with our mother. Of course, she did. This is the day of the reaping.

We know why this works, but in addition to the plot hook and emotional hook already identified, recall that *The Hunger Games* is set in a dystopian future. By contrast, Stephenie Meyer's *Twilight* (2005) at first concerns a teen girl in our world, more or less. She has pretty ordinary teen concerns. As the novel opens, she's on her way to the Phoenix, Arizona, airport to fly north to the wild, rainy Olympic Peninsula in the state of Washington to be with her dad, Charlie.

In the Olympic Peninsula of northwest Washington State, a small town named Forks exists under a near-constant cover of clouds. It rains on this inconsequential town more than any other place in the United States of America. It was from this town and its gloomy, omnipresent shade that my mother escaped with me when I was only a few months old. It was in this town that I'd been compelled to spend a month every summer until I was fourteen. That was the year I finally put my foot down; these past three summers, my dad, Charlie, vacationed with me in California for two weeks instead.

It was to Forks that I now exiled myself—an action that I took with great horror. I detested Forks.

I loved Phoenix. I loved the sun and the blistering heat. I loved the vigorous, sprawling city.

"Bella," my mom said to me—the last of a thousand times— before I got on the plane. "You don't have to do this."

My mom looks like me, except with short hair and laugh lines. I felt a spasm of panic as I stared at her wide, childlike eyes. How could I leave my loving, erratic, hare-brained mother to fend for herself? Of course she had Phil now, so the bills would probably get paid, there would be food in the refrigerator, gas in her car, and someone to call when she got lost, but still …

"I want to go," I lied. I'd always been a bad liar, but I'd been saying this lie so frequently lately that it sounded almost convincing now.

"Tell Charlie I said hi."

"I will."

"I'll see you soon," she insisted. "You can come home whenever you want—I'll come right back as soon as you need me."

But I could see the sacrifice in her eyes behind the promise.
"Don't worry about me," I urged. "It'll be great. I love you, Mom."

Fateful words. *Don't worry about me.* Yeah, right. And why, exactly, is Bella flying to a place she hates? The intrigue is mild, but maybe enough for us to keep going a bit longer.

More interesting to me are the emotional undercurrents in the passage. What is Bella Swan feeling, apart from her conflicting feelings about Forks and leaving her somewhat dysfunctional mom? Are you picking up mixed messages? She's lying to her mother, but she's also lying to us. She's going to Forks for reasons she hasn't yet explained, perhaps for her mother's sake, perhaps to make life easier for her father, perhaps for another reason altogether.

What's buried in Bella's opening narration is anticipation. Of what? We don't know yet, but she does. Things are going to happen in Forks, for sure, but she's in no hurry to tell us what. Instead, we get a dose of the teenage ordinariness, a sense that teens see their parents as hopeless, distant, and out of touch. (In this story, boy, are they!) We also get a hint of inner excitement, masked as *puh-leeze* faux ennui. What Bella is really saying to the reader is, *Once upon a time, in a rainy forest far, far away …*

Bella Swan's yearning is for us to know her, to be in on her secrets, to find out the extraordinary things that are going to happen to this pretty ordinary girl. She may sound like any other self-absorbed seventeen-year-old to us, but what she wants deep down is for us to hear her dark tale.

EMOTIONAL MASTERY 13:
BONDING READERS TO YOUR PROTAGONIST

- The method: Mentally go to your opening moment, or what seems to you a good place to start your story. It's in your mind for a reason.

THE EMOTIONAL CRAFT OF FICTION

- Write down the plot event, however small, happening at this moment, the event that will bring about change and set your protagonist into motion.
- Great. Now cross that out. We're not going to work with that, not necessarily.
- Consider this moment in time and in your protagonist's life. What is something that your protagonist has strong feelings about right now? About whom does your protagonist care? What is something that your protagonist feels matters urgently, or that she doesn't understand? Why? Detail the reasons. Write down what we need to know.
- Your protagonist doesn't just care about this person, situation, or thing; he worries about it. It has implications, not for everyone (though it may) but for your protagonist personally. Write down what your protagonist is afraid will happen to him. Add an aspect of this worry that other people wouldn't know or see. Why is your protagonist able, or unable, to do anything about it?
- Alternately, pick something, or someone, that your protagonist is happy about. What brings her joy? What is she looking forward to? Why is this a good day? Detail why. Add a reason that others wouldn't know or see. Why is your protagonist deserving, or not, of this happiness?
- Whatever passion you are working with, an apprehension or a joy, detail it. Add specifics. What makes this longing unique? Why is it different now than at any other time? Also, what is the experience of this moment like? Create a metaphor. To be in this moment is analogous to … what?
- Is this a perishing moment or a permanent fixture in your protagonist's life? Is it good or bad? How does your protagonist know this is a different experience for him than it would be for anyone else?
- Now take your notes and craft a paragraph or passage that takes us inside your protagonist or shows us what is going on there. Capture not what is happening in the plot, but rather your protagonist's inner yearning.

There are no universal characters but there are universal human desires. Heart. Care. Hope. Dreams. Yearning. From Odysseus to

Meursault (*The Stranger*) to Scarlett O'Hara to Carrie, heroes and heroines capture the idea of human longings that we all feel.

Longing is different than need. Needing to solve plot problems can kick protagonists into action, but that's not the same thing as forging a human bond. What does that is inner yearning.

THE EMOTIONAL MIDPOINT

There are two New York City subway lines I can take to work: The L train or the M train. The M climbs over the Williamsburg Bridge to Manhattan. The L travels beneath the East River.

Most days my first task is to take my son to school or summer camp. If we take the M train, we stand by the sliding door windows and gawk. As the train ascends the bridge, our Brooklyn neighborhood, Williamsburg, grows smaller beneath us. Then we're over the river, still rising, the flat gray expanse of the water below cut by V-shaped barge wakes.

Far off is Oz: towering Manhattan, dense and looming. But we're not there yet. Nor are we at home. As the bridge's apex nears, I try to identify the moment when we're precisely at midspan. It's the high point, the apex, the flex point of the bow. For a split second we're neither leaving nor going, but simply suspended, breathless at the view in both directions. All that came before is falling behind. All that lies ahead still is indistinct.

If we should take the L train, we hop onto the last car of the train. This is so that we can look out the rear window. My son likes to watch for the headlights of following trains, but I like to watch the blue tunnel lights that describe a downward curve of the river approach. Then with a whoosh of pressure change, we're under the river itself. The blue lights end and for a long, dark, and dangerous minute we hurtle down the tunnel tracks, rattling and shaking, as alone as if we were speeding through outer space.

Again, I try to mark the midpoint that is the tunnel's lowest, the nadir, the bottom of the frown. It's a lonely spot. Most commuters distract themselves with iPods, Kindles, Sudoku, newspapers, or paperback classics. I want to dwell, for a bare second, in the blackest moment, when all that is safe is disappearing astern, and everything to come is fraught with unknowns. It's a long ride to the First Avenue station and a breath-exhaling relief when we get there.

And so we arrive at your novel's midpoint, its epicenter and pivot. Do you know which moment this is in your manuscript? If not, it's worth finding. Is it a rise to a hilltop of false promise, or is it a descent into existential despair? Whatever it is, it's a mirror moment: the moment when your protagonist is utterly alone with himself, defined only by hope or dread. It's a second when the story is suspended, unable to go backward and about to plunge forward into the unknown.

There are many ways to use the midpoint. James Scott Bell's *Write Your Novel from the Middle* recommends using it to discover character arc, meaning who your protagonist must become (the end of the arc) and therefore where your protagonist will start (the beginning of the arc).

Many other writers advocate writing the *black moment*, a point of despair from which a new direction will emerge, typically the end of Act Two when all seems lost, but even so, indestructible resolve sets in. ("As God is my witness, I'll never be hungry again!") The black moment might bring a protagonist face-to-face with fear, failure, a dilemma, or death. It might be a moment of truth when a secret is revealed, a protagonist is shamed, or the protagonist's actions are shown to have terrible consequences. (William Styron's *Sophie's Choice* has all of that.)

Whatever the plot or story purpose of the midpoint, it's important to mark it and make space for the reader to experience something akin to the weightless apex of the bridge or the dark nadir of the tunnel. The goal is not to get readers to feel a character's dark night of the soul, but to feel an inner turning and a shift in destiny.

Amity Gaige's third novel, *Schroder* (2013), tells the story of Erik Schroder, a German immigrant, who adopts the name Erik Kennedy as a teenager in 1984 and assumes a new identity as a presumptive (if distant) relative in the famous political family from Massachusetts in order to be accepted at an exclusive summer camp in New Hampshire. Living this lie, he grows up, eventually marries, and has a daughter, Courtney.

Following a divorce, Erik finds his parental rights increasingly limited, so one day during a parental visit he kidnaps his daughter (this moment is not creepy, since they have a nice relationship) and begins a seven-day drive across the Adirondack Mountains region of upstate New York. One evening near Lake George, Erik realizes how irreparable his situation is. He likens himself to a dead man appealing his death, and describes his state of mind:

> But the dead man, his soul in ascension, goes north. I drove a little farther than I had planned. (There's a lot of road up there.) I knew only that to go further from one thing is also to come closer to something else.
>
> Closer, but to what exactly?
>
> Further, but from what?
>
> The guilty mind accelerates, its pedal stuck. Thoughts come with too much velocity. This is its own punishment. Whenever headlights appeared in my rearview mirror, or I saw a car catching up with me from some distance, this velocity took effect. As the lights came closer, filling my rearview mirror, I could not help but drive faster. To speed, like my mind. Only once the cars passed me I would feel myself reeling from the sudden deceleration of my mind. The red glow of the taillights left me nauseous. I knew I was doing something wrong. But many wrong things had been done to me. And sometimes wrong things are done in the service of rightness.
>
> I passed a sign that read, PARADOX, 2 MILES, and laughed bitterly.

Guilty but not yet caught, justified but not really, driving well-marked roads but nevertheless lost, Erik is speeding down the road but is still suspended in time and place. He has neither departed nor arrived. He really can't do either. He's an outlaw. (The novel is a tale told in flashback from a jail cell.)

What Gaige captures here is not exactly a mirror moment. It's not a *good-lord-what-have-I-become*, a *how-did-this-happen*, or an *I've-got-to-change* passage. Rather it's a midpoint, a deeper and more harrowing look down an abyss. It's neither here nor there. It's worse.

There's no hope of getting anywhere. It's a moment of suspension, of pure and terrible being and nothing else. It's a moment without even the relief of judgment. When you've done something wrong, the most horrible thing of all is to be left alone with yourself.

EMOTIONAL MASTERY 14:
THE EMOTIONAL MIDPOINT

- What's the moment of no going back, of despair, of who-am-I-and-what-have-I-become? Note the following: one detail of place, one ache of regret, one brand-new fear, one impossible hope.
- At the midpoint, write down your protagonist's view of herself prior to this time. What about that view is no longer true? Who must your protagonist now become? What is she lacking—and utterly unable to achieve?
- At midpoint, what can your protagonist see (however far off) that was not visible before? What can he no longer see in the distance behind? What is coming? What is never again to be?
- At midpoint, is your protagonist lost or seeing a way forward? Is either condition welcome or unwelcome? What does it feel like to be suspended, lifted out of time, in a moment of pure being? Is this moment sublime or hellish—or both?
- Weave any or all of the above into a paragraph that describes crossing the apex or nadir of the journey.

Has your own life ever reached a turning point? Have you ever had to face up to your mistakes, admit failure, and find a way to go on? Have you ever been wrecked by the knowledge that you are inadequate, that you cannot fix things, or that your limitations are plain for all to see? Was there a moment when you knew you might die in the next few seconds? Has there been a point of do or die, now or never, *it's up to me?*

If you have experienced one of those defining, transitional moments in your life, then you know what you are trying to capture on the page. It's the breathless point when you are poised between two versions of yourself. Things will never be the same again, but even more important, neither will you. What bears the emotion at those times is not what's happening, but the feeling of inescapable devastation and unavoidable decision.

Helpless, swept away, lost, broken, empty, alone. Hurtling onward, unstoppable, still alive, becoming new without even knowing what that means. All of that is the midpoint. This hellish plunge toward death also captures the will to live and, done right, can be pretty emotional.

FAILURE AND DEFEAT

Only one machine stood between us and our goal: bringing our hockey-obsessed son to his first NHL game (Devils versus Sharks) in Newark.

The machine was a New Jersey Transit ticket kiosk in Manhattan's Penn Station. No problem. Ticket kiosks are fast. Slot your card, touch the screen, and you're on your way by rail under the Hudson River. From the Newark station it's an easy two-block walk to the Prudential Center, hockey heaven. Our son was six. His sneakers were hopping with excitement.

I stepped up to the machine. We'd taken a taxi this far. We had plenty of time. I touched the first few screens at the kiosk and then froze.

"Where's my wallet?"

Not in my pocket. In an instant I knew where it was: on the floor of the taxi cab now heading down Seventh Avenue, never to be seen again. I hadn't asked for a receipt. There are a dozen Chase banks within spitting distance of Penn Station, where replacement ATM cards can be obtained in ten minutes, but it was Sunday. They were all closed. I have my American Express number memorized but that was no use. You must slot the actual card.

My driver's license was gone too, plus all my cash. Dash home for a credit card? We live not in Manhattan but far away across yet another river in Brooklyn. It already had taken us forty-five minutes to get this far. At this point the only way back was a long winter walk.

My wife and son stood together looking at me, wide-eyed, waiting for me to explain the solution. Of course I would have a solution. I'm Dad. I always know what to do.

I shoved my right hand into my jeans pocket. Still empty. I checked my back pockets, jacket pockets, the tote bag holding blankets for the ice arena ... no wallet. Without that wallet I wasn't a man. I wasn't even a person. How many times had I passed by panhandlers and scoffed at strangers claiming lost wallets and asking for a dollar for "train fare." Street cons.

No one was going to help us. It was all up to me, and my pockets were empty. I had no ideas. I didn't even have any change. My wife doesn't carry her wallet when she's with me, and we were a long way from home.

My son said, "Dad?"

I raised my eyes. Above me there was only a fluorescent light fixture. What could I possibly say?

Well now.

Have you ever had the floor fall away beneath your feet? Have you ever been deflated or defeated? Have you ever been robbed? Have you ever had a mirror held up to you, one relentlessly honest?

Has a spouse or partner walked out of your life for good? How do you feel at those times?

Not only betrayed, but naïve. Not only shamed, but helpless. Not only victimized, but trampled. Not only punctured, but broken. At those times, the foundations of your life and the floor under your days are gone. Presumptions that surround your existence are no longer true.

So it is with characters. The past is erased. The future is a void. What a character—what anyone—feels is not only insecurity, loss, or grief. It's the end of identity. Not just a moment of reckoning but a hurtling over a cliff. Moments of defeat may turn around later, but for a time it feels like the end of the story. It's got a power out of proportion to the actual event. It's a foretaste of death.

What's the worst thing that happens to your protagonist in your current novel? What's the worst defeat, the final one? Does it have the feel of finality?

Chevy Stevens's harrowing debut novel, *Still Missing* (2010), is a story that is bound to take us to such a place. It's the story of Canadian real estate broker Annie O'Sullivan, who finds herself alone at the end of a workday. A potential buyer shows up at the last minute at the house she's showing—and abducts her. For a year Annie is held prisoner in a hideously well-thought-out prison—a small house deep in the unpopulated forests of Vancouver Island. Chained, starved, beaten, and repeatedly raped, Annie becomes pregnant and gives birth to a baby girl. The baby immediately contracts pneumonia, which her abductor—whom Annie only refers to as The Freak—refuses to have treated.

Still Missing, which is written as a series of letters to Annie's psychiatrist after her escape, handles the baby's death this way:

> To this day no one knows my baby's name—not even the cops. I've tried to say it out loud, just to myself, but it stays locked in my throat, in my heart.

When The Freak walked out that door with her body, he took everything left of me with her. She was only four weeks old when she died—or was killed. Four weeks. That's not enough time to have lived. She lived nine times longer in my belly than she did in the world. I see pictures in magazines of kids the same age as she would be now, and I wonder if she'd have looked like them. Would her hair still be dark? What color eyes would she have? Would she have grown up to be happy or a serious person? I'll never know.

My clearest memory of that night is him sitting at the foot of the bed with her in his arms and I think, Did he do it? Then I think even if it wasn't intentional, he killed her by refusing to get any help for her. It's easier to hate him, easier to blame him. Otherwise I go over and over that night trying to remember how she was lying when I last placed her back in her bed. For a while I'll convince myself that she was on her back and it was my fault because she probably had pneumonia and drowned in mucus. Then I think, no, I must have placed her on her stomach, and I wonder if she smothered while I lay sleeping not five feet from her. I've heard that a woman is supposed to know when her child is in trouble. But I didn't feel anything. Why didn't I feel it, Doc?

Worse than defeat itself, perhaps, is feeling helpless in defeat. That's how Annie O'Sullivan remembers the death of her baby daughter. *But I didn't feel anything.* It's a moment of helplessness and self-blame so profound that the only possible emotional response is numbness, pure emptiness.

But is Annie feeling true emptiness? Look again. Stevens captures this bottomless feeling of defeat by filling the passage with emotional cues. *What color eyes would she have?* The absence of feeling is conveyed through feeling, paradoxically, which is then denied, or more precisely, suppressed because the feeling of defeat itself is unbearable.

Enormous failures, big defeats, and black moments are good, of course, but as in life there are, or can be, moments of challenge, reckoning, betrayal, setback, and coming up short in fiction. What happens to your protagonist's sense of self at each of those moments? Each is an opportunity.

In the story I told at the opening of this section, what delivered the gut punch? Perhaps it was my son, so eager to see his first NHL game, looking at me and asking, "Dad?" There you have it.

The punch is not in the event itself (losing a wallet) but in the intangible thing that is lost (a kid's faith in Dad). At any other time, losing my wallet would just be annoying. That Sunday—this is a true story—it was more.

I was going to let my son down.

I was going to fail as a dad.

It was a death.

EMOTIONAL MASTERY 15: FAILURE AND DEFEAT

- Go to the middle of your manuscript. Look at your protagonist. Pick a moment of challenge, reckoning, betrayal, setback, or coming up short.
- For your protagonist, what's the worst part of this situation? What makes it excruciating? What makes it a personal failure?
- Work backward in the story to set up the moment and why this particular kind of failure should hurt so much. Who is counting on your protagonist? Who is let down? What is the most painful way in which we can see that disappointment?
- What depends on your protagonist succeeding? What is slipping out of reach? What does it feel like to let that go? (Create an analogy.)
- At this moment, what does your protagonist wish she could do instead? What does your protagonist wish she could say, but can't?
- As your protagonist fails in the moment you've chosen, involve others. When the floor falls away, let it fall away in a public place.

Oh, one more thing: Small failures can deliver little deaths, but they can also deliver little triumphs, too. That Sunday at Penn Station, we made it to the hockey game after all. Dad pretty quickly recovered his cool. Mom happened to be carrying an ATM card, too. The moment was handled. But, oh! For a minute there, it was the worst. I was about to fail as a dad. But I didn't.

Dad had a trick up his sleeve for that situation: She's called Mom.

CATALYST AND CATHARSIS

When was the last time you blew your top? For me, this isn't a particularly difficult question to answer—did I mention that I'm a dad? When my kids push me over the edge, the transgression often is, in the great scheme, a trivial one. A year from now will I care? A decade from now?

No, probably not.

And yet, *ka-boom!*

There's something interesting about my explosions, though. If they are big enough, they result in a "family talk." Mostly that means Mom and Dad talking sternly. The kids say less, but more often than not they reveal the hidden reasons for their misbehavior. Thanks to my explosion, the lid is off. Confessions, needs, and secret fears come tumbling out. Bad behavior becomes understandable. Solutions arise. We accomplish something.

Another way to say it is that the explosion releases the truth. Kids who cannot express themselves except through nonverbal actions suddenly find their words. The explosion clears a space. The worst has happened and so, paradoxically, the family now becomes a place of safety. The explosion has somehow given us all strength.

We're talking about catharsis. Notice two things about catharsis: There is a catalyst and there is a consequence, often a positive one. There's the match that lights the fuse and the new freedom that follows the bang.

In your work in progress (WIP), what is the catalyst event that causes the seething pot of your protagonist's inner conflicts to boil over? How does your protagonist act out? What is released? Who else is affected? What change results?

You used to be able to count on Stephen King for fear, but these days you can count on him for much, much more: a full range of emotional experience from one of our greatest storytellers. His novel *Joyland* (2013) is a beach read potboiler about New Hampshire college student Devin Jones, who, dumped by his girlfriend and feeling despondent, takes a summer job at a theme park called Joyland. The park is haunted (quite literally) by a long-ago murder in a funhouse ride. Though he cannot get over his ex-girlfriend, Devin rotates jobs in the park and learns the lingo and lore of the carny types who are its permanent staff.

What shakes Devin out of his funk and sets him on the road to redemption is an unexpected event on opening day, when, for the first time, he wears the suffocating character costume of Howie, the park's dog mascot. Amid the hectic swirl he sees a line of little kids being led toward a day-care building, Howie's Howdy House, where they are left so their parents can enjoy lunch at the park's class-A restaurant, Rock Lobster. Ditched by their parents, the kids are terrified. Some are crying. The "Hokey Pokey" is playing over the public address system.

> Buried in the Howie costume, looking out through the screen mesh that served as eyeholes and already sweating like a pig, I thought I was witnessing an act of uniquely American child abuse. Why would you bring your kid—your toddler, for Christ's sake—to the jangling spray of an amusement park only to fob him or her off on a crew of strange babysitters, even for a little while?
>
> ...

I didn't know what to do either but felt I had to try something. I walked toward the line of kids with my front paws up and wagging my tail like mad (I couldn't see it, but I could feel it). And just as the first two or three saw me and pointed me out, inspiration struck. It was the music. I stopped at the intersection of Jellybean Road and Candy Cane Avenue, which happened to be directly beneath two of the blaring speakers. Standing almost seven feet from my paws to furry cocked ears, I'm sure I was quite a presence. I bowed to the kids, who were now all staring with open mouths and wide eyes. As they watched, I began to do the Hokey Pokey.

...

I put my left foot in; I put my left foot out; I put my left foot in and I shook it all about. I did the Hokey Pokey and I turned myself around, because—as almost every kid in America knows—that's what it's all about. I forgot about being hot and uncomfortable. I didn't think about how my undershorts were sticking in the crack of my ass. Later I would have a bitch of a heat-headache, but just then I felt okay—really good, in fact. And you know what? Wendy Keegan never once crossed my mind.

Devin saves the kids from their fear, and in a real sense saves himself from despondency. It's a cathartic moment from which Devin can move forward. He leaves his broken heart behind and progresses toward solving the murder mystery, seeing the ghost in Horror House, and encountering a local single mother, whose son David, in the terminal grip of muscular dystrophy, is the eerily prescient character who elevates this breezy coming-of-age novel to a level of mystical terror. Catharsis dancing the Hokey Pokey in a dog costume?

Well, why not?

If you are Stephen King, catharsis can be found in the most un-expected places.

- What frustrates your protagonist? What inner need is constantly thwarted? Find three new ways to increase the need and one way in which to punish your protagonist for having that need.
- When you hammer, defeat, deny, or humiliate your protagonist, what about that so enrages your protagonist that he would pick up a gun, heedless of the cost or consequences?
- What's the biggest way in which your protagonist can act out? What can she destroy? Whom can she attack? What's the most hateful or most truthful thing she can say? What will shock others in the story?
- Having spent himself, what can your protagonist—or someone else—now do that he could not do before? What is now permissible to say? Show that.

Many manuscripts lack a true catharsis. Perhaps novelists are afraid of it because it's scary, messy, and hard to clean up. The truth, though, is that in life, catharsis happens all the time, in big ways and small. Cathartic moments are as necessary as breathing, doing your laundry, or having a good cry.

The same is true in stories. So go ahead, explode. Or let your protagonist do so. We'll all feel better; trust me.

SCENES IN WHICH NOTHING HAPPENS

Imagine you're having a holiday dinner at home. A tablecloth is spread. Silverware is laid. All is perfect until you knock over a glass of red wine. What happens? Quickly you spread open a white table napkin and drop it over the spill. The puddle of wine seeps through.

The tablecloth is now, in a way, a memory. The napkin is a map of the little lake of wine. The wine is infused in both. Even after you throw them in the wash the stains remain, faintly, as a reminder of a meal that started long ago and, in a way, is never finished. The memory is there forever.

Perhaps you know some laundry tricks that I don't know? Or you use paper tablecloths and napkins? Never mind. You get my point. When you infuse something as strong as red wine into an absorbent piece of cloth, a faint awareness of that wine lingers. Future meals are infused with and informed by the memory of that small holiday disaster.

Your novel is like that. It's the dining room, a place where many meals are eaten and finally add up to a story. Every one of those meals, though, involves that tablecloth and napkin, which are imprinted with something that I would call your protagonist's greatest need. That need is always present even if you cover up that stain with a table runner and cleverly fold the napkin. You know it's there. You are always aware of it.

Have you come across scenes in excellent novels that seem to have little plot but work anyway? Have you ever felt the undertow of a character's yearning in commonplace action, pulling your awareness down below the surface of an everyday situation? Such scenes are infused with the point-of-view character's fundamental, underlying and, as yet, unmet need. That need, and its tug, twists, and turns are what is happening when plot is on hold.

There's a nice example toward the beginning of David Leavitt's *The Indian Clerk* (2007), which begins at Cambridge University in 1913 and is the story of mathematician G.H. Hardy, whom, at thirty-seven, has become one of the great mathematicians of his age. Hardy receives a handwritten letter from an obscure clerk, Srinivasa Ramanujan, in the accounts department of the Port Trust Office in Madras. The letter, in which Ramanujan requests help in getting published, is full of mathematical formulae, some nonsensical, some bizarre, and some utterly brilliant. Frustratingly, proofs are not provided.

Hardy and his sometime partner in publishing, Littlewood, decide that there is enough promise in Ramanujan's letter to bring him to Oxford and assist him. This is done, with some difficulty. Ramanujan is different than expected, but also clearly working on a high level, mathematically speaking. His way of thinking is different, unschooled, culturally strange, and wildly creative. Hardy is drawn to him, even though there is a mighty distraction in the world with the arrival of war with Germany:

> [Hardy] tries, as much as he can to see Ramanujan. Standing in shadowed profile before the river, his arms folded behind his back and his stomach protruding slightly, he might be the silhouette of a Victorian gentleman, cut from black paper and pasted against a white ground. Restraint and discipline, a certain aloofness, or perhaps even elusiveness: these are his most distinguishing traits. Except when they're talking mathematics, he rarely speaks except when spoken to, and when he is questioned, almost always answers by dipping into what Hardy envisions as a reserve of stock replies, no doubt purchased on the same shopping trip in Madras during which he was supplied with trousers, socks, and underwear. Replies such as: "Yes, it is very lovely." "Thank you, my mother and wife are well." "The political situation is indeed very complex." Here he is, after all, in English clothes and on English land, and still Hardy can't begin to penetrate his carapace of cultivated inscrutability. Only occasionally does Ramanujan let something slip, a whiff of panic or passion slips through (Hobson! Baker!), and then Hardy feels the man's soul as a mystery, a fast-moving prickle beneath his skin.
>
> Mostly, those afternoons, they talk mathematics.

Why is Hardy so fascinated by Ramanujan, and frankly bothered by the man's opaque inner life? Is it because Ramanujan may be the man to devise the proof that has preoccupied Hardy his entire life, the Riemann hypothesis? Is it because Ramanujan is mysterious and elusive? Is it because he is exotic, Indian? Is it because Hardy is "that way" (homosexual) and that Ramanujan reminds him of an Indian cricketer at Oxford after whom Hardy lusts?

It could be any or all of that. I would say, though, that it is because Hardy is a man whose work is understood by perhaps only twenty people, half of whom are in Germany, now the enemy. And he's a man who feels distant from his own collaborator and dissatisfied with his social circle, the distinguished and famous members of a stuffy semisecret society. It is because he is lonely. Hardy longs to connect. That longing is not stated as such; instead, it's felt through his close observation of Ramanujan and his wish, somehow, to break through the man's reserve.

When nothing seems to be happening, plenty can be happening. Perhaps it's going on below the surface, but it's there nonetheless. It's a tension that's not public but personal, a need that pulls at your protagonist, an emotional ache that causes us, in our own ways, to ache as well.

EMOTIONAL MASTERY 17: WHAT'S HAPPENING WHEN NOTHING IS HAPPENING

- Identify your protagonist's greatest inner need, the one that would preoccupy your protagonist even if your novel's plot were never to come about. Craft a sentence or short paragraph that succinctly expresses that need.
- Pick out a scene from the middle of your WIP. Try to make this a minimally dramatic scene. Open a new document on your computer screen. Paste in the sentence or paragraph you created. This is the opening of a new version of the scene you've selected.
- With the underlying need just below the surface of your protagonist's awareness, rewrite the scene. Do not look back at the version in your WIP!

- The purpose of this rewrite is to get your reader to feel the underlying need in your protagonist. Work until you're sure we will sense that need even though you don't mention it or make it plain.
- Finally, go back and delete the paragraph you pasted in at the scene's start. How does the scene feel now? Is the underlying need coming through even without being spelled out?

EMOTIONAL GOALS IN SCENES

Similarly, scenes that are more active on the surface can keep us reading solely because of their underlying emotional tension. If there's no plot problem in place in a given scene, yet we avidly read anyway, it may well be that what's keeping us gripped is an underlying and unmet emotional need, an emotional goal.

Molly Gloss's novel *Falling from Horses* (2014) is the story of plainspoken Bud Frazer, an Oregon ranch hand and occasional rodeo cowboy, who in 1938, at the age of nineteen, boards a bus for Hollywood to find work as a stunt rider in Western movies. Seated on the bus next to him is twenty-one-year-old Lily Shaw, who is also Hollywood bound, hoping to be a scriptwriter. While the novel covers a year in their lives in Hollywood, their relationship begins on that bus.

At first they are just seatmates—two kids who've never been far from home, embarking on the first big adventure of their lives. But they are also young and single. What do we expect will happen? Gloss plays with our expectations this way:

> I didn't have a lot of experience with girls, but it crossed my mind that she might think I was sneaking looks at her under cover of looking at the mountain; I thought she might be wondering whether I found her pretty. She wasn't pretty, at least by my standards back then. She had thick dark eyebrows that just about met over her nose—

she hadn't yet begun to pluck them—and she was so skinny there was nothing to fill out the front of her wrinkled dress. Plus the dress was bright green with an orange collar, which might have looked all right on the right girl, but it threw an orange pallor onto her face. I didn't have any interest in her, not in that way, but I figured I had better be clear about it. So I said, "I wonder if you'd mind switching seats. I like looking out at the country going by."

Falling from Horses has a flashback framework, told decades after the events of the novel. We know from the opening that Bud worked as a stunt rider for only a year and later became an artist specializing in Western subject matter. Lily went on to a major career as a screenwriter, had multiple marriages and lovers, testified at the McCarthy hearings in the fifties, and wrote a memoir. But on this bus ride they are newbies to everything, including to each other and to love. So what do we anticipate?

What actually happens at this point, romantically speaking, is nothing. Is Gloss teasing us? Bud denies being attracted to Lily; indeed, he tells us that she wasn't pretty. Is Gloss whetting our appetite? Perhaps. We'll find out, but meanwhile we sense, I believe, that Bud has an unspoken emotional need even more fundamental than the obvious one: He needs a friend. That need begins to be fulfilled on the ride, as we see a short while later:

> Lily stuck with her reading for a while, and anyway, being Lily, she wouldn't have admitted to nerves, but we were taking the curves pretty fast, and when she closed the folder of pages and asked me where I was from and where I was headed, I figured it was to take her mind off the curvy road and the likelihood of our bus plunging into the gorge. I don't know if that's right—she has written otherwise—but it's what I thought at the time.
>
> I told her I was going down to Hollywood to work in the cowboy movies, which caused her to perk up slightly. She said she was headed there too, to get into the business of writing for the movies.

She asked if I was an actor, and I told her I was just expecting to ride in posses and such, which wasn't really acting. Then I told her what I'd heard—that the work was mostly riding fast and pretending you'd been shot off your horse. She had never been on a horse in her life, but she'd seen enough cowboy movies to know what I meant. "You might have to jump onto a runaway buckboard to save the girl," she said, "and maybe shoot the gun out of the bad guy's hand." She said all this with a straight face—she had a dry sense of humor and never liked to give away that she was joking. It wasn't exactly a test, but if I'd taken her for serious I imagine she might have decided I was too dumb to bother with.

Now, tell me that Gloss isn't teasing us! Lily's remark about saving the girl has to be a piece of foreshadowing, doesn't it? Plus there is the metaphor of falling off horses, and Bud's self-deprecating suspicion that Lily might regard him as nothing more than a dumb cowboy with Hollywood stars in his eyes. Something's cooking, but what exactly? If nothing else it's a connection, a friendship, which at this point is what Bud and Lily need more than anything.

Bud doesn't tell us what he needs emotionally, and Gloss is too skillful to lay it out, yet her protagonist's yearning is all too evident. At this moment we don't know the twists and turns that Bud and Lily's relationship will take, but we hope that these two starry-eyed kids will connect and support each other, which in fact they ultimately do, for many years. Bud's emotional goal is to find a friend, and in Gloss's restrained and yet warm opening, he does.

In classic formulas of scene construction, the first decision is to set a protagonist's goal. What the protagonist wants to get, do, discover, or avoid is the outward goal, the visible objective of the moment, but just as important is the protagonist's invisible objective, the emotional goal that matters to his heart. In some cases it's the only goal.

EMOTIONAL MASTERY 18: EMOTIONAL GOALS IN SCENES

- Look at the scene you're writing right now. Who is the point-of-view character? At this moment in the story what does that character have to do, get, seek, or avoid? This is commonly called the scene goal.
- Shift focus. What does your POV character need inside? What does she hope to feel? That's the emotional goal.
- What in this scene is pulling this character closer to or farther away from the emotional goal? What is making that emotional goal impossible to achieve? How does this character attempt to reach the emotional goal in spite of what's happening?
- Add to that. Why is this character afraid of his emotional goal? What can he do to subvert or avoid it? Conversely, why does the emotional goal greatly matter? What can make it matter more?
- In this scene, how does this character reconcile to the loss of the emotional goal, or to gaining it? What replaces it? What comes next? How is the scene's outcome more satisfying, or less acceptable, than what was originally hoped for?
- Finally, take the raw material you've created and fashion a passage that tells, and/or action that shows, your character's inner state in this scene. Make the point of the scene to capture the dynamic inner "me" as much as to shift the outer circumstances of the story.

EMOTIONAL BREAKTHROUGHS: GETTING REAL

While we're here, let's have a look at the opposite of unspoken need: suddenly getting real.

In a conversation with a friend, have you ever said, "I know what you're about to say." In a social or work situation, have you ever thought to yourself, *I know what's really going on here!* Have you ever called someone out? Have you ever cut through the BS and told it like it is?

If you have, then you know that what transpires on the surface isn't always what's really happening underneath. Human interactions are layered. Someone may be asking for a cruller at a Dunkin' Donuts counter, but the brisk demand and the American Express Platinum card flicked over for payment mark this as an assertion of status. The tow truck driver who demands two hundred in cash to haul the stalled BMW of the Dunkin' Donuts customer to the garage that's only two hundred yards away is doing the same thing, but in reverse. People play status games.

As powerful as the unexpressed undertow of need can be in a scene, the moment when a true need or reality underlying a situation breaks through to the surface can be equally as forceful. Call out. Cut through the clutter. Remove the masks. Confess. Get down to brass tacks. Tell it like it is. There's force and emotional effect in sweeping away artifice and exposing the raw reality that we usually try to ignore.

Getting real is what happens when a scene's subtext bursts through. Any sudden shift in tone, unexpected openness, challenge, show of force, sudden softening, begging for compassion, or other call to genuineness and honesty can become electrifying and emotional. We don't show our true colors lightly. Telling the truth of things is risky. When a character is honest or humbled, that moment recalls for us the moments when we, too, have had to stop pretending, quit acting, show our true selves, and get real.

Getting real is both terrifying and refreshing, and it can happen at almost any point in a novel, because characters are pretty much always concealing themselves from each other, readers, and you, the author. If you're unsure what's hidden and what can emerge from a character, you only need to demand this: *For cripes sake, get real a second why don't cha?* What's been boiling inside turns into steam;

and it's steam, you may recall, that turns turbines and generates power. When characters suddenly get real, we connect with them and, with relief, feel our own facades crumble.

Kristin Hannah's *The Nightingale* (2015) is about two French sisters in World War II: one who fights in the Resistance, and one who stays home in the country and must battle in different ways. The sister who stays home, Vianne Mauriac, must say goodbye to her husband, who has been mobilized, and then she goes to stay with her childhood friend, Rachel de Champlain. The two try to converse normally, making the best of their new situations, but the tension of the times breaks through:

> Rachel moved the infant to her shoulder, patted his back soothingly. "Marc is no good at changing diapers. And Ari loves to sleep in our bed. I guess that'll be all right now."
>
> Vianne felt a smile start. It was a little thing, this joke, but it helped. "Antoine's snoring is a pain in the backside. I should get some good sleep."
>
> "And we can have poached eggs for supper."
>
> "Only half the laundry," she said, but then her voice broke. "I'm not strong enough for this, Rachel."
>
> "Of course you are. We'll get through it together."
>
> "Before I met Antoine ..."
>
> Rachel waved a hand dismissively. "I know. I know. You were as skinny as a branch, you stuttered when you got nervous, and you were allergic to everything. I know. I was there. But that's all over now. You'll be strong. You know why?"
>
> "Why?"
>
> Rachel's smile faded. "I know I'm big—statuesque, as they like to say when they're selling me brassieres and stockings—but I feel ... undone by this, V. I am going to need to lean on you sometimes, too. Not with all my weight, of course."
>
> "So we both can't fall apart at the same time."

"Voilà," Rachel said. "Our plan. Should we open a bottle of cognac now, or gin?"

I'm not strong enough for this. It's a heartbreaking confession, a worry, and foreshadowing. It's also a step closer to the scary reality that they will soon know. Our hearts open to Vianne, and fly to her—or is it that their hearts fly to us? Either way, we feel the weight of war descending.

EMOTIONAL MASTERY 19: GET REAL!

- Stop at any point in your manuscript. Who is the POV character? Address this character like a New York City cop: Stop right there! Whadda ya think you're doin'? What's really goin' on here? C'mon, talk!
- Stop at another point in your manuscript. Who is the POV character? Become Mother Teresa: My child, you are suffering. Our Father in Heaven understands and forgives all. Tell me what's troubling you. What do you need? What do you wish to confess?
- Stop at another point in your manuscript. Who is the POV character? Become Oscar Wilde or Dorothy Parker. Slam this character with a withering truth, a devastating irony, a shot straight to the psychological solar plexus.
- Stop at another point in your manuscript. Who is the POV character? Become the Oracle of Delphi: You wish to know your destiny? I will tell it to you, but be warned: If it pleases you, beware, and if it displeases you, be overjoyed. Ready? Your future is …
- How can you use any of the results above to pierce through the fog, crack the artifice, and suddenly get real?

Emotional plot follows patterns that do not appear in your synopsis and that cannot be summarized in a *Publishers Weekly* review. Its conflicts are not easy to see and its scenes are invisible. A *get real* moment is a turning point in an emotional scene. It undermines our expectations and either collapses the emotional scene like a building demolition or lifts it to a higher plane like a lock in a canal lifts a barge.

When we feel that collapse or lift, it tells us that we're in the midst of a struggle that has nothing to do with the plot. It's the struggle of characters to maintain lies about themselves, to avoid the truth, and, finally, to discover that it's not possible to fool others and ourselves forever. Sooner or later we have to get real. That sudden burst of honesty is a step in the emotional plot, the conflict that truly grips us.

PLOTTING THE NON-PLOT-DRIVEN NOVEL

Have you ever grown impatient with a novel? Have you ever restlessly flipped ahead wishing that something would *happen?* Of course. It's a common feeling. Put politely, you feel frustrated. Put plainly, you're bored.

Perhaps your own current manuscript has also had you feeling, at times, impatient. Have you struggled to find a way to come up with events dramatic enough? Is your main character in turmoil, yet has nothing terribly special to do? Do you secretly worry that your beautiful words won't be enough to captivate your readers for four hundred pages?

If you answered yes, then I have bad news for you: Your readers are going to feel impatient, too. Not enough *is* happening. But what can you do about that? In particular, how can you "plot" a novel that inherently lacks one?

Even more, how can you work alchemy when your process is exploratory, the opposite of applying a formula? As a non-plot-driven novelist, your frustration can deepen when you consider classics and contemporary literary successes. *To the Lighthouse. The Bell Jar. The Remains of the Day. White Teeth.* I mean, come on. What really *happens* in these novels? Almost nothing, and yet somehow it feels like everything.

There's nothing wrong with writing about the human condition. It's okay to examine characters who are stuck. You could say this about Holden Caulfield, John Yossarian, Jay Gatsby, and even Scarlett O'Hara, all characters who are not getting what they want. Yet writers like Salinger, Heller, Fitzgerald, and Mitchell make it look easy. Fortunately, there are ways to plot the non-plot-driven novel. It doesn't mean creating an outline. It doesn't depend on the gimmicky formulae of quest, save the world, whodunit, or love conquers all.

It does, however, require taking a break from writing pages and asking yourself questions about your main character. First, recognize that a non-plot novel needs to hold together over its length, but it also needs to provide some kind of tension in every scene. Also, if your novel doesn't, and cannot, have a plot, then you are likely to be working with a main character who is blocked, frozen, hamstrung, bewildered, wandering, lost, or in some other way unable to become whole and happy.

Stuck characters are a challenge. They too easily become passive. Instead of acting, they react. When they are weak and without agency (the ability to act), they become depressing to read. Okay, so what are you supposed to do when there's no demon to slay, murder to solve, or homestead to save? What is your protagonist supposed to do when he is frozen, blocked, bewildered, lost, or wandering?

When your protagonist has no problem other than being stuck, the action of the novel needs to be about getting unstuck. What gives the non-plot novel its narrative tension is not what needs to get done, but the things that need to change. It's not to save the world, but to transform the self.

Outward events can trigger that transformation, but the transformation itself takes place inside. That is deceptive. Change needs a catalyst. Also, in life, change is evident to those around us. We act differently.

Notice the word "act"? That means actions that we can see, speech we can hear, and objectives that we can measure progress toward.

Change that happens only inside isn't really change. Change is meaningful if we can show it, interacting differently with others and in the world. Change is attempted, rehearsed, tested out, tried on. It's an active process. That's true in fiction, too.

The pattern of change can be a slow, rising resistance that builds up to an explosive release, or something else. It can be a deliberate plan to be different (one that fails), a conflict projected onto others, or a destructive force that forces your protagonist to grow. Writers tend to think of change as a singular event, but change is most effective when it involves ongoing struggle. That's how it is in life, isn't it? We understand ourselves better and change a little every day, so why shouldn't characters change a little in every scene, too?

The approach I'm recommending plays off your readers' feeling of impatience. If you think about it, that impatience is expressed not only as *I wish something would happen*, but as unspoken questions like these:

- Why can't the protagonist just get what he wants?
- Why can't she simply talk it out?
- Why can't he just walk away or quit?
- Why can't she simply change?
- No, seriously, why not?

Now let's adapt those questions in two ways and use them in two contexts. First, with respect to your manuscript as a whole, reframe the questions like this:

- What big thing could my protagonist do to get what he wants?
- What big thing has to happen before underlying conflict can be talked out?
- Who (not what) is actively holding back my protagonist?
- My character can change, but before that she must go through what?

The answers to those questions lead us to the outward, visible, practical things that your protagonist needs to do. They suggest the people with whom your protagonist has conflict, or from whom your protagonist must get something. They imply that there are places to go, projects to complete, calamities to avoid, people to pursue, or symbolic activities that represent the struggle inside. Change is not easy. If it were simple, then the first set of questions would be unnecessary. There would be no novel.

But luckily change is hard. There's stuff your protagonist must go through. That stuff makes up the events that enact the story. If that stuff can be summarized or boiled down or revolve around one big thing, then that thing is premise, the framework of your non-plot-driven novel, the ballgame, battle, hoopla, enterprise, exploit, excursion, conduct, deed, stunt, risk, trial, rumpus, run-in, coup, crusade, venture, push, passion, gamble, or any other activity that will be summarized in reviews and cause film producers to see a movie in your novel.

A framework is nice, once you have it, but there's still a long middle to get through. There are a score or more of scenes that need to deepen, develop, and complicate things. How can you make those active? It's simple. Just add two key words to each of our previous questions:

- What could my protagonist do—*right now*—to get what he wants?
- What's getting in the way—*right now*—of talking things out?
- Who—*right now*—is holding back my protagonist and how?
- My character is avoiding herself for what reason—*right now*?

In a way, it doesn't matter which scenes you choose to write. Every one of your choices has an answer to one of the above questions buried in it. That in turn leads you to what can occur to enact, show, dramatize, and make outward your answer. Something can always *happen*; you simply must identify why.

EMOTIONAL MASTERY 20:
PLOTTING THE NON-PLOT-DRIVEN NOVEL

- Considering your protagonist's overall experience in the time frame you intend for your novel, ask the four big questions:

  1. What big thing could my protagonist do to get what he wants?
  2. What big thing has to happen before underlying conflict can be talked out?
  3. Who (not what) is actively holding back my protagonist?
  4. My character can change, but before that she must go through what?

- Work with your answers. Of the things your protagonist could do, what is holding her back? Whether it's a test, trial, or experience to go through, what is the biggest obstacle? Which is the hardest? Which will demand the most? Which stirs up the most issues inside?
- Focus on that one element. Distill it. Make it bigger, more colorful, more unusual, more singular. Twist it. Turn it upside down so that it's in some way different from, or even the opposite of, what we expect.
- How can that element become the core of your protagonist's experience? State it as a problem, a conflict, or a journey—toward what? Your novel may be about many things, but, simply put, this one element—expressed in this way—is your premise.
- For each scene in your manuscript, ask the four big questions:

  1. What could my protagonist do—*right now*—to get what he wants?
  2. What's getting in the way—*right now*—of talking things out?
  3. Who—*right now*—is holding back my protagonist and how?
  4. My character is avoiding herself for what reason—*right now*?

- What your protagonist could do right now is this scene's objective. What's getting in the way is this scene's conflict. Who is holding your protagonist back is this scene's antagonist. The reason for avoiding self is this scene's inner conflict.

- Make the objective intentional. Make the conflict more complex. Make the antagonist determined, clever, and more powerful, righteous, and resourceful than your protagonist. Make the inner struggle impossible to settle. Make it altogether more difficult for your protagonist to get through the scene.
- With those things in place, you have a goal, obstacles, an antagonist, and inner conflict, the basic structure of a scene.

We like to think or imagine that non-plot-driven novels can be successful because of their beautiful writing. We want to believe that their authors have found, or have been born with, a certain magic—the magic of conjuring novels out of nothing.

It's true that language alone can create a certain tension in readers that keeps them apprehensive, but that tension is fleeting and almost impossible to sustain over four hundred pages. Characters tend to be reactive in novels where beautiful writing is the author's primary value and main offering. It's possible to make reaction vital reading, but, again, for readers that's thin nourishment. At a certain point hunger sets in—hunger for the visual, the active, the changing.

When we feel strongly, we feel strongly. When something makes us feel extremely passionate, we act. Characters are the same, only more so. When you or I would freeze, they spring. Where you or I would suffer, they do not stand for it. What is mysterious to us is a mission to them. Where life throws things at us, they throw things back. We have dreams; they have destiny.

That's why you're writing about them.

THE READER'S MAP

When there's no plot, as such, how is the reader supposed to measure the progress of a story? Without an outward goal to strive toward, how do we know which direction we ought to be going and how far we've come? What's the destination? Without a conventional plot won't the reader get lost?

Won't the writer?

Readers need maps. They need a guide to good and bad. They need a mental graph to help measure your character's wants, worries, progress, and ideas of what's important. They need a compass to point them, a trail to follow, milestones to reach, and scenic outlooks where they can survey the story world and marvel at your creation. They need to apprehend the whole forest, not just experience the trees.

Then again, those trees are important. Nailed to them are the trail markers. You find them at the story's bends. Each one is different. Come across a trail marker and you know you've reached a point on the story's map. String them together and you have a trail. Trails in turn lead somewhere: the destination or outcome that we hope to reach. That's especially important when obvious plot markers are absent.

This is not to say that a novel needs to be literally mapped out or rendered like a schematic diagram. For both writers in writing and readers in reading, look only at the map and you'll miss the pleasures of the trail. Look only at the markers and you'll miss the grandeur of the map. What's ideal is when readers feel a sense of progress in a story without knowing why. When a story both feels like it's unfolding to a plan and like at any moment it could deviate from the expected, that's perfect.

Charlie N. Holmberg's gaslamp fantasy *The Paper Magician* (2014) faces this challenge. It's the story of Ceony Twill, a new graduate of the Tagis Praff School for the Magically Inclined in an alternate London. Ceony dreams of an apprenticeship in powerful metal magic but is instead assigned to the lowest, least glamorous, and most ephemeral form of the art, paper magic. Once she is bonded to paper, it will be her only magic, for life, so Ceony is understandably less than thrilled.

She goes to apprentice with the surprisingly young, cheerful, and gifted paper magician Emery Thane. Much of the novel concerns Ceony's apprenticeship in paper magic. Out of that Holmberg must devise a plot. There is Ceony's bias to overcome, of course, and her teacher, Thane, has dark secrets that devolve into a dangerous rescue in the novel's second half. Still, the plot elements are not plentiful. How then does Holmberg convey a sense of story progress? How do readers mark Ceony's inner journey—not only her discovery that there is far more to paper magic than she supposed, but also her growing commitment, her growing attachment to Thane, and a sense that what's happening matters?

Thane is a mentor, which helps greatly. Through Thane, Ceony not only learns, and learns to care, but also develops an appreciation of the significance of a type of magic that seemed to comprise little more than parlor tricks, though Thane's parlor is indeed highly amusing. When Ceony brings her first book to life, a children's book called *Pip's Daring Escape*, with ghostly images in the air, she is astonished, yet still dismissive:

> Ceony's throat choked with words. "Wh-What? I did that?"
>
> "Mm-hm," Mg. Thane hummed. "It helps when you can see an image, such as with picture books, but eventually you'll be able to read novels and have those scenes play out for yourself, if you wish. I admit I'm impressed—I thought I'd have to demonstrate first. You seem familiar with the story already."
>
> Once again she flushed, both over the praise and over being called out for having read what, in her mind, was a childish thing. The ghostly images lasted only a moment longer before fading away, as all unread stories were wont to do.
>
> Ceony shut the book and glanced at her new teacher. "It's ... amazing, but I admit it's also superficial. Aesthetic."

"But entertaining," he combated. "Never dismiss the value of entertainment, Ceony. Good-quality entertainment is never free, and it's something everyone wants."

Ceony's sense of paper magic's significance continues to deepen through her apprenticeship, and it's through that mechanism that her story seems to deepen, too. Paper magic comes to mean something to her. It's not her growing skill but her growing understanding that marks the stages of her inner journey. Holmberg takes it in steps and is careful to choose, mark, and measure those steps as we read.

EMOTIONAL MASTERY 21: THE READER'S MAP

- At your story's end, what is the destination that your protagonist will reach, and who is already there? Work backward. At the beginning, send a message from that person.
- At your story's end, what will your protagonist get? Work backward. At the beginning, give your protagonist a taste of that prize.
- At the story's end, ask your protagonist what was surprising about the journey. Work backward. At the beginning, make your protagonist's world one in which such things do not happen.
- At the story's end, ask your protagonist what hurt the most along the way. Work backward. At the beginning, hint that your protagonist is especially vulnerable in this way.
- At your story's end, who will your protagonist become? Work backward. At the beginning, set a different and misleading desire as the goal.
- In your current scene, what's a tiny detail of the setting that has big meaning for your POV character? Pause to examine it.
- Pick a random spot in the story. What's your protagonist's inner condition? Experience it like a place. Get it down in words.
- Along the journey, at what point does the map run out? Pinpoint the moment and work until there are no options, no detours, and no help. At that moment your protagonist should be well and truly lost.

- There is a compass for every journey. What is the inner compass that your protagonist needs to reach her destination? Make the compass impossible for her to find, and yet right in her pocket.

The journey is more than the map and more than the trail. It's both. Your characters have much to experience, but it's also important how they experience their story. What is the map inside your main character? Progress along the inner path is measured not by how close or far away your protagonist may be from an external goal, but by delving deeply into each step of the journey. Slow down to dwell in each moment and readers will paradoxically sense the story's urgency speeding up.

To put it differently, when you take time for your protagonist to feel lost, to wonder, or to measure meaning and study self, the need to arrive somewhere grows and with it a sense of that destination lying ahead. The more the journey itself matters, the more its outcome also does. As a reader, don't you love it when you want a story to hurry up, but also never to end? That's the emotional dichotomy that you want readers to feel. Applying the methods of the reader's map is how to achieve that effect.

THE TRUE ENDING

Romance writers have an acronym for endings: HEA, meaning Happily Ever After. Hero and heroine have united. Troubles are over. A wedding can happen and, once the vows are said, there will no longer be serious conflict. Thriller writers, meanwhile, save the world. Mystery writers enact justice. Fantasy writers finish the quest. Women's fiction writers bring wholeness and healing to their heroines. And that's all we want, right? For things to be okay. When they are, the story is over.

Right?

Well, not quite.

What is it that brings human beings peace? Lasting, deep down contentment, satisfaction, well-being, and fulfillment? Partly it is self-acceptance. That's the job of the inner journey. Solving problems is matched by a transformation inside. Inner struggle is complete, and a new person steps forward. Not only are plot problems resolved, but a protagonist achieves wholeness too. But that's only part of true peace. What comes after plot resolution and personal growth? Healing the world.

Each of us cannot be truly at peace until the rest of us are, too. That's why we put dimes in cardboard slots for charity, clear litter from highways, serve on church committees, march in Washington, blog about important issues, bust up fights, buy shoes for needy kids, sponsor impoverished children in Peru, pray, walk for the cure, and walk on the moon. We are not at peace until we not only care about things, but also do something about them and make a difference. We are world citizens.

When the world becomes a better place, we become better people. Our satisfaction is deeper. Our contentment turns to hope and our fear of death diminishes. In story terms this means that the job is not finished at HEA, the happiness of your protagonist, but when we know that everyone else in your protagonist's world will be okay, too.

In chapter four, I mentioned M.R. Carey's *The Girl with All the Gifts*, the story of a ten-year-old female *hungry* (zombie) trapped in the Echo Hotel, an experimental facility. The kids are taught in order to see how well they learn (very well, as it happens), but there is one special teacher whom the novel's heroine adores: Helen Justineau. She treats the kids like children instead of lab rats. She tells them stories and plays her flute. At the end of the novel, most of the adult humans meet an appropriate fate, but Helen survives. And having been granted life, what does she do? In the novel's final scene, entirely safe in an environmental protection suit, she teaches young hungries the alphabet.

I could include a method of Emotional Mastery here, but I think you know what to do. The highest human good is not gaining happiness, but giving back. Happiness brings a smile and gladness of heart, and that's fine, but selfless actions bring joyful tears and enduring gratitude. So think of it this way: Have your protagonist change your world—your fictional world—and you will change your readers, too.

CHAPTER SIX

The READER'S EMOTIONAL *Journey*

Certain moments in life are a sure bet for tears. Graduation, college send-offs, breakups, vows at a wedding, goodbyes at the airport, the death of a pet. These are transitions. A long span with a loved one comes to an end. A treasured time of happiness is over. Letting go is necessary, and maybe for the good, but it's difficult. Why can't things stay the same? Why can't that which is beautiful and precious go on forever?

Other occasions are guaranteed to induce rage. Someone hurts your child. Your partner has an affair, or lies about one. You get ripped off. That conniving so-and-so at the office gets undeserved credit. An unjustified traffic ticket is awarded. Injustice is served. Blameless people undergo bad things.

Fear comes in many forms, too. The adrenaline stab as your car spins on ice. The dread of being summoned to the boss's office on a day when the company is downsizing. The phone message to call your doctor immediately. Feeling lost in a strange city, a pounding on your door, a dark garage, a sharp sound that indicates someone is in your house.

Tears, rage, and terror are big, but notice that when they occur they are preceded by something. They come about when conditions are right. They also carry with them attendant feelings. Sorrow is most acute when happiness is ending. Farewell is all the more poignant when coupled with gratitude. Rage is made worse by helplessness. Fear is the greatest in anticipation of the blow, not as the hammer hits.

Big emotional experiences are engineered by circumstances. When the right factors line up, we cannot help but cry, pound our fists, or scream. Since we know what stirs up such feelings, why not use those factors in fiction? Why not force the circumstances that guarantee big emotions for readers?

Is it wrong to manipulate readers? Says who? Stories are meant to stir us—we see that every day. News broadcasts spin reality to shock us. Ads invoke our fears and touch our soft spots. Politicians and preachers affirm our beliefs and make us yearn for a better world. Our feelings are affected by stories all the time, so why not use those same means on your readers? Stirring hearts is your aim.

As mentioned earlier, readers turn to fiction precisely to have an emotional experience. They want to be blown away by stories and changed by the novels they choose. You can write your story and hope to have that effect on your readers, or you can craft a story to make sure that it does.

Your choice.

Let's have a look at some known ways to affect readers' emotions. Some of them may be useful, not only to captivate readers and keep them coming back for more, but also to serve your story's purpose. The exact purpose of your story doesn't matter to me, not at the moment. What matters is whether or not you make readers receptive to your purpose by opening their emotions. You may think of that as manipulation, but if the point you're making is a good one, then I'd say the means are justified.

HIGH MOMENTS

Elsewhere I have argued that certain types of story events create high moments, and these moments are ones that move our hearts. They're ones we always remember. Of those highly emotional events these are the durable ones: forgiveness, sacrifice, betrayal, moral dilemma, and death.

Let's check out some examples.

FORGIVENESS

Jason F. Wright's *The Wednesday Letters* (2007) is an unusually structured novel. It's a series of letters written over the course of forty years, every Wednesday, from a husband (Jack Cooper) to his wife (Laurel). After Jack and Laurel die, the letters are discovered by their children, who read them in random order and discuss them as they discover their parents' story.

It's a story of courtship, marriage, war memories, travel, Graceland, money woes, births, the Cubs, elections, fireworks, church, holidays, and a horrible secret of which the children were ignorant (spoiler alert): In 1959 their mother was raped. Not only that, the rapist repented. And became a pastor. And with Jack and Laurel's help, became *their* pastor.

Are you kidding me? This act of forgiveness on Jack and Laurel's part is hard to swallow (as some readers have said in Amazon reviews), and so it falls upon Wright to explain how such a thing could happen. In one of the letters, Jack describes to Laurel his experience at a courtroom parole hearing for the rapist three years after his prison sentence began:

> They had me speak first, which I opposed, but it didn't matter. I told them word-for-word what I've been telling you for three years. That three years just isn't enough time. There's no way to know if he'll stay away from us, if he'll stay sober, if he'll be any different than the day he went in.
>
> The other witnesses told about his redemption, about how far he'd come, but I don't want to believe any of it. I don't want to forgive. I want him to drink tonight, to make a mistake, to leave the state, to be arrested for disorderly conduct. I won't want him to hurt someone else, I just want him to hurt himself.
>
> I want him back in jail for so long that you and I will have left this earth before he sees the other side of the fence.
>
> His attorney said he deserved another chance. She talked about their visits and his journals. He's been memorizing scriptures, and said he deserves a chance to finish finding God. To help others. To be a man again.
>
> I wish I hadn't spoken first.
>
> I cannot deny to you or God what I saw. He was not a different man, but he is surely changing. When they asked him whether he thought he should be released, he said that he knew he wasn't perfect, he said he'd never be, and that he would make mistakes again. But he said he'd accept their decision and live by it. He cried when he said he was sure that whether in prison or in the world, he would spend every hour of every day of this life paying and repenting for that moment of drunken evil.
>
> Then he said something that surprised me. He said that he'd never again make a mistake that would hurt another. It was compelling. It was, or at least seemed, heartfelt.
>
> Laurel, I want to hate him, for you. That somehow seems natural and right and allowed. I want to see him suffer, balled upon the

THE EMOTIONAL CRAFT OF FICTION

floor, crying and screaming for rescue. I want no one to rescue him. I want to let him lie there forever.

But at that moment, in that room, all I saw were clean and sober eyes. All I felt as they granted him parole was pity and remorse. He's trying. You're trying. I'm not.

God forgive me.

-Jack

Forgiveness is hard to give, but it's even more painful not to give. Forgiving is important to do. It's in the Bible. It's in the Qur'an. It's in novels like Khaled Hosseini's *The Kite Runner*, Lisa See's *China Dolls*, Kristin Hannah's *Night Road*, and shines in novels like Alan Paton's *Cry, the Beloved Country*. It's imperative in life and in stories, but its emotional power clobbers readers for a reason that we don't at first see.

Whatever your feelings about justice, whether you are an offender or a victim, whether you can forgive or you need time yet to heal, Wright's passage reminds us that the act of forgiveness is a fundamental change that occurs, most important, in the one who must forgive.

SACRIFICE

When we think about sacrifice, we tend to think about the ultimate sacrifice: giving one's life for another. Literature is full of such noble sacrifices: Sydney Carton in *A Tale of Two Cities* ("It is a far, far better thing that I do, than I have ever done ...") and Robert Jordan in *For Whom the Bell Tolls*, for example. But there are many levels of sacrifice. Small sacrifices can be as touching as big ones.

Richard Paul Evans, author of the best-selling inspirational novel *The Christmas Box*, doesn't take it easy on his characters. In *The Walk* (2010) he gives his arrogant Seattle advertising executive, Alan Christoffersen, the perfect life: a perfect home, perfect career, and perfect wife, McKale. Then, like God does to Job in the Bible, Evans takes it all away. McKale is thrown from a horse, paralyzed, and dies. While that's happening, Alan's business partner steals the company. Alan's home goes into foreclosure. Despondent, Alan decides to walk all the way across the country, to Key West, to reckon with himself. This is a journey that will take him five volumes, completed with *Walking on Water* (2014).

The Walk only takes Alan across the state of Washington, where he passes roadside chapels and churches that leave him bitter. He sleeps outdoors. He is attacked. Late in the novel he comes upon the cutely themed 59er Diner with a row of bungalows behind it. A kind waitress, Ally, befriends him and arranges for him to rent a bungalow. That evening she knocks on his door, brings him a selection of sandwiches (meatloaf and a Spanky's Clubhouse) with baked potato, onion rings, and a chocolate-chocolate malted milkshake with extra malt.

They have a thing about malt in Washington State, I know, but Ally brings Alan more than just food. They talk. Alan tells her his story. She tells him a little about herself and a town down the road, Leavenworth, which is a faux-Bavarian hamlet. Then she invites him to the sofa, but not for the reason we might expect:

> "I bet. How are your feet?"
>
> "Sore."
>
> "Come here." She stood, took my hand, and led me to the sofa. "Sit," she said. I sat down, and she sat cross-legged on the floor in front of me and untied my shoes.
>
> "You sure you want to do that?" I asked.
>
> "Absolutely. If you don't mind, that is."
>
> "I won't stop you."
>
> She pulled off my shoes, then began to gently knead my feet. "Tell me if I'm doing it too hard or too soft."
>
> "It's just right," I said.

THE EMOTIONAL CRAFT OF FICTION

For several moments we both sat in silence. I couldn't believe how good it felt to be touched. I laid my head back and closed my eyes.

"Tell me about yourself," she said.

"I just did."

"That was your former self. No one goes through all you went through without changing."

I opened my eyes. "What do you want to know?"

"The real stuff. Like, what are you going to do when you reach Key West?"

"I don't know. Maybe just keep walking into the sea."

"Don't do that," she said.

"What else do you want to know?"

She thought for a moment. "Do you believe in God?"

"There's a question," I said.

"Does it have an answer?"

"Let's just say I'm much too angry at Him not to."

"You blame God for what happened to you?"

"Maybe. Probably."

She frowned, and I could tell that what I said had bothered her. "I didn't mean to offend you."

"You didn't. I just wonder why it is that we blame God for everything except the good. Did you blame Him for giving her to you in the first place? How many people go through their whole lives and never get to experience that kind of love?"

I looked down.

It's pretty hard to miss the parallel to the biblical story of Mary washing the feet of Jesus with tears, her hair, and perfume (Luke 7:38). Spanky's Clubhouse sandwich doesn't have the same poetic heft, perhaps, but the point is that Ally cares enough to sacrifice a bit of her time, a substantial amount of the diner's food, and a whole lot of her wisdom to bring Alan a new perspective: gratitude, rather than bitterness, toward God.

Alan changes and so do we. The stuck-up advertising man whom we were tempted to feel deserved a takedown is as loved by God as we. The lesson for storytellers is that sacrifice can be big or small; what makes sacrifice moving is not its size but how much it is needed.

BETRAYAL

What about betrayal? Kristan Higgins's hilarious *Too Good to Be True* (2009) is the story of a single woman, Connecticut schoolteacher and Civil War reenactor Grace Peterston. (Yes, really, a Civil War reenactor. And, yes, it's funny.) Grace has a colorful family (her mother sculpts female genitalia), a gay best friend, a cute dog, and a bad habit of making up boyfriends, especially now, since her ex-fiancé is still around and currently dating her beautiful younger sister Natalie. Grace adored her younger sister, so much so that when baby Natalie was brought home from the hospital, she thought Natalie was a birthday present.

Naturally, we get the backstory of Grace, her ex-fiancé, Andrew, and the end of their engagement just mere weeks before their wedding: "Grace ... there's something we need to talk about," he says. "You know I care about you very much."

Uh-oh. Everyone knows what that means, and so does Grace.

> "I'm so sorry, Grace," he whispered, and to his credit, his eyes filled with tears.
>
> "Is it Natalie?" I asked, my voice quiet and unrecognizable.
>
> His gaze dropped to the floor, his face burned red, and his hand shook as he ran it through his soft hair. "Of course not," he lied.
>
> And that was that.
>
> ...
>
> Natalie was wrecked when she found out. Obviously, I didn't tell her the reason for our breakup. She listened to me lie as I detailed the reasons for our breakup ... just wasn't right ... not really ready ... figured we should be sure.

THE EMOTIONAL CRAFT OF FICTION

She asked only one quiet little question when I was done. "Did he say anything else?"

Because she must have known it wasn't me doing the breaking up. She knew me better than anyone. "No," I answered briskly. "It just ... wasn't meant to be. Whatever."

Natalie had no part of this, I assured myself. It was just that I hadn't really found The One, no matter how deceptively perfect Andrew had looked, felt, seemed. Nope, I thought as I sat in my newly painted living room in my newly purchased house, power-eating brownies and watching Ken Burn's documentary on the Civil War till I just about had it memorized. Andrew just wasn't The One. Fine. I'd find The One, wherever he was, and, hey. Then the world would know what love was, goddamn it.

Natalie finished her degree and moved back East. She got a nice little apartment in New Haven and started work. We saw each other often, and I was glad. It wasn't like she was the other woman ... she was my sister. The person I loved best in the world. My birthday present.

Ouch. Some gift. Higgins ironically plays against Grace's feelings of betrayal, which only makes her sister's Judas kiss feel more foul. It isn't the act of betrayal that's so bad; it's who does it, and how.

MORAL DILEMMA

A dilemma is a choice between two equally good or two equally bad outcomes. A moral dilemma elevates such a choice by giving two outcomes equally excellent, or excruciating, consequences not only for a protagonist, but for others. A dilemma is a situation in which none of us likes to be caught, but in which we all sometimes find ourselves. A moral dilemma is a situation nobody wants, and which few must ever face, but which is terrific for making compelling fiction.

Thanks to its title, Liane Moriarty's *The Husband's Secret* (2013) would seem to be about secrets, but in fact it is a long tale of a woman caught in a moral dilemma. (Big spoiler ahead.) The woman in question is Sydney housewife Cecilia Fitzpatrick, who searches the attic for a piece of the Berlin Wall (obtained in her youth) because one of her daughters is studying the subject in school. In the attic she finds a sealed letter from her husband, which he's marked to be read only in the event of his death. However, he is not dead.

Whether or not to read her husband's letter is a fine dilemma, but Cecilia's dilemma grows worse when she actually reads it: It's her husband's confession that, at the age of seventeen, he murdered a girl who jilted him, Janie Crowley. Now, what would you do? Turning her husband in to the police would be legally correct, but Cecilia's husband, John-Paul, is father to their two daughters. And the fact is, she loves him.

Still, John-Paul murdered Janie Crowley. The girl's mother, Rachel, is still alive, working as a secretary in a school. Rachel believes, erroneously, that Connor Whitby, now a physical education teacher at the school, is the one who murdered her daughter. We readers know that is unfair; John-Paul is the killer.

Moriarty deepens Cecilia's dilemma by piling up the reasons for Cecilia to rat on her husband. Or not. When confronted, John-Paul is remorseful and admits he's a coward for not turning himself in. He's now a dad and understands what he did to Janie's parents. Remorse does not excuse John-Paul, but it does make it more difficult to turn him in. In the key scene in which Cecilia first confronts John-Paul over the letter, their daughter Polly awakens in the night. John-Paul puts her back to bed. Cecilia has just adjusted to the realization that her husband is evil, but then:

> "She's gone back off," said John-Paul. He was back in the study, standing in front of her, massaging little circles under his cheekbones, the way he did when he was exhausted.
>
> He didn't look evil. He just looked like her husband. Unshaven. Messy hair. Shadows under his eyes. Her husband. The father of their children.

If he's killed someone once, what was to stop him from doing it again? She's just let him go into Polly's room. She's just let a murderer go into her daughter's room.

Just it was John-Paul! Their father. He was Daddy.

How could they tell the girls what John-Paul had done?

Daddy is going to jail.

For a moment her mind stopped completely.

They could never tell the girls.

"I'm so sorry," said John-Paul. He held out his arms uselessly, as if he wanted to hold her but they were separated by something too vast to be crossed. "Darling, I'm just so sorry."

Cecilia wrapped her arms around her naked body. She trembled violently. Her teeth chattered. I'm having a nervous breakdown, she thought with relief. I'm about to lose my mind and that's just as well, because this cannot possibly be fixed. It is simply not fixable.

The reasons to turn in John-Paul and the reasons not to turn him in continue to pile up in Moriarty's novel until Cecilia's inability to choose takes so long that a tragedy happens: The vengeful mother of the murdered girl, Rachel, is finally able to attempt revenge on the PE instructor, Connor, whom she erroneously blames. Instead of hurting him, though, she injures Cecilia's innocent daughter Polly. In the wake of that horrible mistake, the truth of Janie Crowley's murder becomes known and, interestingly, Rachel then finds herself caught in a dilemma not unlike Cecilia's. She could turn in John-Paul, the true killer, and justice would be complete—but was her own fit of violent rage, which resulted in Polly's injury, really any different?

Dilemmas create emotional anguish for characters, which in turn challenges readers to consider what they would do if the dilemma were theirs. Our anguish may not be as acute, as we're one step removed, but we twist our hands anyway. That is, we twist them if the dilemma is truly difficult.

Dilemmas, then, work best when the stakes are both high and personal. When one choice is morally right, it will win out unless it is offset by a different choice that is equally compelling in personal terms. Law versus love. Tell the truth or protect the innocent. Be honest or be kind. When there's no way to win in a story, the winner is us.

DEATH

What is better than capturing the poignancy of death? Crassly put, when readers are sobbing, cash registers are ringing. You'd think that sorrow would be a turnoff, a feeling readers would avoid, but everyone loves a good cry.

Sometimes.

Under the right conditions.

The operative word here is *good*. What causes us to want to cry, to feel happy that we are sad? Sadness by itself is not a feeling that we want, certainly, but sorrow is. Sorrow adds something to sadness. Sorrow happens when we have not only lost someone, but also *miss* them. Their absence isn't emptiness, which is final, but a feeling of incompleteness. When death is sad, it is a door closed; when death triggers sorrow, the door is still open. But to what? To something good that we don't want to give up. To a person we care about. And the more we care, the greater will our sorrow be.

Thus, when we consider sob-fest fiction like John Green's *The Fault in Our Stars* (2012), which is about teenagers dying of cancer, we need to look at *not* how the author handles the teenagers' dying, but how he portrays the way they live their lives. If we love being with them while they're alive, we'll be wrecked when they die.

The narrator of *The Fault in Our Stars* is Hazel Grace Lancaster, an Indiana teen who has lung cancer. She's been living with death for a while and is firm in her contempt for the soft language and medical bromides that are supposed to help her cope. As the novel opens she is depressed. "But, in fact," she writes, "depression is not a side effect of cancer. Depression is a side effect of dying." Tell it like it is, Hazel! Already we are cheering for this clear-eyed seventeen-year-old.

Hazel's contempt, which is a side effect of her struggle to come to terms with an adversary she can't defeat, finds an easy target in The Support Group, a kids-with-cancer club that meets in a church basement. Augustus Waters, a young writer with the offhand gravitas of Jack Kerouac and the profound wit of a teen Cole Porter, also joins this pointless weekly exercise in seeking positivity in doom. Augustus drives horrifically, has lost a leg, and dangles from his lips a cigarette that he never lights.

Plus, he's hot. And even more impossibly, he's knocked out by Hazel, who herself is no slouch in the wit-before-dying department. In their first support group meeting together, Hazel decides for the first time to speak up, quoting from a book she reads obsessively, *An Imperial Affliction*, by Dutch author Peter Van Houten, who will later figure significantly in the plot:

> I looked over at Augustus Waters, who looked back at me. You could almost see through his eyes they were so blue. "There will come a time," I said, "when all of us are dead. All of us. There will come a time when there are no human beings remaining to remember that anyone ever existed or that our species ever did anything. There will be no one left to remember Aristotle or Cleopatra, let alone you. Everything that we did and built and wrote and thought and discovered will be forgotten and all of this"—I gestured encompassingly—"will have been for naught. Maybe that time is coming soon and maybe it is millions of years away, but even if we survive the collapse of our sun, we will not survive forever. There was a time before organisms experienced consciousness, and there will be time after. And if the inevitability of human oblivion worries you, I encourage you to ignore it. God knows that's what everyone else does."

I learned this from my aforementioned third best friend, Peter Van Houten, the reclusive author of An Imperial Affliction, the book that was as close a thing as I had to a Bible. Peter Van Houten was the only person I'd ever come across who seemed to (a) understand what it's like to be dying, and (b) not have died.

After I finished there was quite a long period of silence as I watched a smile spread all the way across Augustus's face—not the crooked smile of a boy trying to be sexy while he stared at me, but his real smile, too big for his face. "Goddamn," Augustus said quietly. "Aren't you something else."

She is, and that's the point. Hazel and Augustus are impossibly expressive for teens. He is a poetic dreamboat with one leg. She is a sardonic goddess with an oxygen tube. They fall in love, travel together to Amsterdam to meet Peter Van Houten, and throw eggs at passing cars. Augustus quips sarcastically of their church basement meeting room, "We are literally in the heart of Jesus," but it's clear that it's Augustus who is Hazel's salvation. When death comes at the novel's end, the last hundred pages of the book might as well be printed on Kleenex so we can rip out each page and blow our noses.

To make death poignant, make living beautiful. To make us miss characters who will die, make them the very best thing about being alive.

EMOTIONAL MASTERY 22: PUSHING HIGH MOMENTS HIGHER

- Does your protagonist (or someone else) need to be forgiven? What did he do? Look at the one who must forgive. Work to make that a person for whom this particular act of wrongdoing is unforgiveable.
- Keep working with the person who must forgive. In what way is that person someone who needs to change more than anyone else? In what way? Why is that change impossible? What would make that person relent?

- Who is someone in your story who can make a sacrifice, big or small? Work not with that character, but with the other person for whom the sacrifice will be made. Make that someone whose need is tremendous.
- Keep working with the need. Build it up. Tear down other avenues of help. When things are at their worst, the time is ripe for the sacrifice.
- Will your protagonist be betrayed? Work the most with the one who will do the betraying. Make that someone important to your protagonist. What is the worst way for the betrayal itself to come to light? Make the pain acute.
- Find a choice that your protagonist must make. Build the choices until each is so necessary that there is no way to choose, no way to win. Keep working until the choice is impossible.
- Who in your novel will die? Cause us to love that character more. Does death pervade your novel? Make living beautiful. Fill the story with joy, and love.

SYMBOLS

We all know about symbols, obvious and invented. Will waving the flag ever get old? Will red roses and diamonds ever fall out of favor? Cross, crown, stars, eagle, dove, torch, poppies, cherry blossoms, barber poles, disco balls, masks, shamrocks, the caduceus … We are surrounded by symbols and take them for granted. They had to start somewhere, though, and gained their meaning because of historical use, which is suggestive for fiction writers. Anything can be turned into a symbol.

Symbols are not only objects; they can be gestures, places, and words. Story can be symbolic all on its own, as in allegory. Considering the power of this oldest of literary devices, I'm surprised that so few contemporary novelists use it. Maybe they are afraid of being obvious, cheesy, or artless, or maybe they just forget. Whatever the reason, symbols have an undeniable effect on readers and deserve more respect.

The effectiveness of symbols begins with their setup. If there is no context, as with diamond rings, symbols can have no effect. For readers to discover the symbolic meaning of an object they must be exposed to it in a pattern. Symbols sneak up. They're perhaps not noticed at first, and aren't meant to be, but after some recurrence, the note they strike is recognized. That isn't always the way, of course. Big symbolic actions are the most potent when they come out of the blue.

Cathie Pelletier sometimes writes as KC McKinnon, as with her 1999 novel *Candles on Bay Street*. Set in a town in northernmost Maine, Fort Kent, right where Route 1 begins near the Canadian border, this novel is the story of veterinarian Sam Thibodeu. Sam's partner in his veterinary practice is his wife, Lydia, but he still harbors feelings for his high school crush, the wild Dee Dee Michaud, who back in 1982 took off with a local bad boy. When Dee Dee returns to town with her nine-year-old son, Trooper, Sam's feelings are reignited, much to the amusement of his wife, who promptly makes herself Dee Dee's best friend.

Sam's feelings are sidelined when it becomes clear that Dee Dee has returned to Fort Kent not only to open her candle-making business on Bay Street, but (spoiler!) because she is dying. Furthermore, she has two requests of Sam: 1) raise her son Trooper once she's gone, and 2) help her end her life. Sam is a veterinarian. He knows how. The drugs needed are available in Canada, just over the bridge. Sam struggles with the decision but ultimately decides to help her die. He obtains the drugs. They choose a night for her death. Sam and Lydia spend that evening with Dee Dee and Trooper, but they are not the only ones:

> "Come on," Dee Dee said finally, when it seemed like the stillness between us would crack and break, like glass. "This is a party," she said, "I want to see smiles on those faces." In the candlelight, the dark circles under her eyes had disappeared as if by magic.

THE EMOTIONAL CRAFT OF FICTION

"Dee Dee," I said. I had made up my mind to say something, about people, about the foibles of human beings. We couldn't go on all night long pretending. But I didn't have to say anything. Trooper bounded suddenly from the window.

"Sam," he yelled. "Come look!" I went to the window. As far as I could see, all the way down Bay Street, dots of fire were bouncing up and down in the night air.

"What the hell is going on?" I asked Trooper. I still couldn't decipher what I was seeing. It looked like hordes of cigarette lighters at a Bruce Springsteen concert. Then I realized what was happening. Dozens of flickering candles were bobbing in the darkness. People were coming from up and down the street, people were coming from all over town, to 204 Bay Street, each holding a candle in his or her hands. I saw Ross at the vanguard, with Vickie. As Dee Dee's front yard quickly filled, it looked like a huge field of fireflies lighting up the night. And above the candles were the faces of the townspeople. They were the people who knew Dee Dee since she was a little girl. They were her new friends, her students from the candle-making class. They were the bartenders at Bee Jay's, the waitresses from the café, even strangers. It seemed to me that half of Fort Kent was there. They had come from all over town to say goodbye with candles. These were candles they had bought from her. Or candles she had taught them how to make. They had come to say goodbye to a wild and crazy girl, a girl they had grown to love.

Once you have opened a new box of tissues to replace the one you have used up reading this tear-jerker ending, you might be asking yourself: *Is that too much? Come on, talk about cheesy! The whole town turns out to say farewell to a suicide? With candles?* If you are asking yourself such questions, take a look at the tissues in your wastebasket. *Candles on Bay Street* became a Hallmark movie, probably because of that very scene. Cheesy? If it works, it works. Why not go for what is emotional?

Symbolic words become meaningful in an altogether different way. Their significance strikes most sharply not when heard in a familiar context but when they leap out of one context into another, as in the ironic reversal of a term of affection. "Nice fart, Princess, are you proud of yourself?" Or, "We love you, you know that don't you, Shithead?" Poetic and metaphoric terms can recur, become labels, and turn into shorthand. Symbolic words don't sneak up on us; a spotlight shines on them.

Australian author Graeme Simsion's worldwide bestseller, *The Rosie Project* (2013), concerns a professor of genetics named Don Tillman, who hilariously refuses to see what is perfectly obvious to everyone else, that he suffers from a profound case of Asperger syndrome. He is ridiculously smart, comically organized, and completely clueless about people. Nevertheless, at the age of forty he decides to have one last go at finding a life partner. He devises a scientific method for finding the perfect mate: a twenty-page (single-spaced) questionnaire that he dubs The Wife Project, which he asks candidates to fill out.

The results, as you might expect, are not excellent.

Then, graduate student Rosie Jarman, who is in every way wrong for Don, stumbles into his life. She is disorganized, emotional, a smoker, and always late. Their initial encounters go badly, even though Don volunteers to help Rosie with determining the identity of her birth father by using genetics. By midnovel, Don's questionnaire does turn up a nearly perfect match for him in the form of Bianca Rivera ... perfect, that is, except for one thing: Bianca is a champion ballroom dancer. Don, a very quick study, sets about to teach himself ballroom dancing in ten days, memorizing and practicing the steps to every style of dance using a biology department skeleton as his dance partner.

However, Don has neglected something: To dance, one must recognize the beat of the music. When the time comes at a faculty ball to dance with Bianca, Don blows it and becomes a laughingstock, a familiar situation to him. Rosie rescues Don by leading him to the dance floor and giving him a cue from the movie *Grease*. *"Dance,"* she says, *"Just fucking dance."* Having memorized the Grease routine, Don and Rosie triumph.

Later, Don shares a taxi ride with Rosie, which he deems a sensible use of fossil fuel. In the dark she asks him the color of her eyes. He knows: brown. They share confidences about her cold stepfather and his dead sister.

Then …

> The taxi driver coughed artificially. I presumed he wasn't asking for a beer.
>
> "Do you want to come up?" said Rosie.
>
> I was feeling overwhelmed. Meeting Bianca, dancing, rejection by Bianca, social overload, discussion of personal matters—now, just when I thought the ordeal was over, Rosie seemed to be proposing more conversation. I was not sure I could cope.
>
> "It's extremely late," I said. I was sure this was a socially acceptable way of saying that I wanted to go home.
>
> "The taxi fares go down again in the morning."
>
> If I understood correctly, I was now definitely far out of my depth. I needed to be sure I wasn't misinterpreting her.
>
> "Are you suggesting I stay the night?"
>
> "Maybe. First you have to listen to the story of my life."
>
> Warning! Danger, Will Robinson. Unidentified alien approaching! I could feel myself slipping into an emotional abyss. I managed to stay calm enough to respond.
>
> "Unfortunately I have a number of activities scheduled for the morning." Routine, normality.
>
> Rosie opened the taxi door. I willed her to go. But she had more to say.
>
> "Don, can I ask you something?"

"One question."

"Do you find me attractive?"

Gene told me the next day that I got it wrong. But he was not in a taxi, after an evening of total sensory overload, with the most beautiful woman in the world. I believed I did well. I detected the trick question. I wanted Rosie to like me, and I remembered her passionate statement about men treating woman as objects. She was testing to see if I saw her as an object or as a person. Obviously the correct answer was the latter.

"I hadn't really noticed," I told the most beautiful woman in the world.

Notice how in this passage Simsion sets up a symbolic phrase on the fly, "the most beautiful woman in the world," and then immediately has his protagonist use it in a devastatingly ironic (not to mention self-destructive) way. *"I hadn't really noticed," I told the most beautiful woman in the world.* Ouch! Don, you doofus! We cringe and die a little inside, wishing and hoping that this Asperger's-plagued professor could somehow overcome his handicap and take the hand of a woman who is clearly falling in love with him.

Words do emotional work, when you work them properly.

EMOTIONAL MASTERY 23: SYMBOLS

- What's a place in the story with heart significance? Burn it down, then build it again.
- What's a relationship that matters to your protagonist? Damage it, then repair it.
- What's an object that holds memories for your protagonist? Lose it, then find it again.
- What's a word with special meaning for your protagonist? In how many ways can you use it in the story?

- Go to your climactic scene. Where is that set? What's an object in that place that only your protagonist would notice? Plant that same object or others like it earlier in the manuscript, building up its symbolic value.
- In your story, will your protagonist (or anyone else) forgive or be forgiven? What's the most visible and meaningful way in which that can happen? Earlier, enhance the meaningfulness of that gesture, that place or those words. Take away, in some fashion, what later will be given back.
- For your protagonist, what's the most significant demonstration of love? What's the keenest sign of loss? What's the warmest welcome? What's the ugliest gesture of contempt? What's the biggest signal of celebration? Set up the symbolic whatever-it-is earlier in the story.
- What's an idea or belief that's the opposite of what your protagonist thinks or believes? Pick or create a character who will embody that opposite. How? Overdo it. Don't worry about being obvious. It's unlikely you'll be told to scale it back.

Symbols are more than flags, eagles, roses, rings, lockets, lightning, rain, or snakes. Anything meaningful to your characters can reverse, recur, or be deployed in ways that enhance its significance. Characters themselves can represent an idea, a belief, or a particular aspect of human nature. The meaning of symbols isn't inherent. It's a meaning that you make—and you can make it out of anything.

STORY WORLDS WE DON'T WANT TO LEAVE

Did you ever have a day that you wanted to go on and on? What made that day so magical? Was it where you were, who you were with, or that particular time in your life? Perhaps, but I doubt it.

Why? Because you've probably been "there" before and since. You've likely been with that person or those people at other times. There were, by necessity, other days in that era in your life. None of those factors are by themselves what caused that particular day to be so magical.

Now let's admit that your wedding day was special. It's not (I hope) ever going to happen again. But if you think about it, it's not the vows, but other things that made that day so amazing. The assembly of so many people important to you. The focus on you. The pictures that will last forever. The security. The support. The love. The ring. The relief. The music. The permanence. The happy ending and happier beginning. The feeling that now everything is going to be okay.

Even one-of-a-kind occasions like weddings reveal that it's not the place, the people, or the occasion that produce the feeling of wanting a day to go on forever. What makes the *day* feel that way is the way that *you* feel. It's not what's happening outside, but what's happening inside.

That has implications for creating a story world that is magical, absorbing, vivid, and involving, and a place readers don't want to leave. Our feeling of wanting to linger isn't generated by the setting itself, by lovable eccentrics in your cast, or by what happens to your protagonist—though those things aren't bad. The feeling of wanting to linger comes from *our* feelings.

If it was as easy as laying cobblestone streets, filling bakeries with chocolate eclairs, dispensing warm wisdom from the mouths of colorful secondary characters, and giving your main characters blue eyes and nice manners, well then, heck, we'd all know what to do: cobblestones, chocolate, wisdom, and blue eyes and *voilà*, you'd have a fictional place that your readers won't want to leave. But that's not it. We long to stay when we are swept away by emotion.

How is that done? There's no formula or checklist. Instead there is the challenge of giving your readers an emotional experience, one that's generated by factors other than the place.

Let's explore.

Go back to that wedding day. One of the things that made that day special was the *relief*. Ever wonder why people smile, applaud, and dab tears of joy during the recessional back down the aisle? One reason is that two people finally made it to the altar and said the vows. The parents' jobs are at last done. No one choked. No one tripped. The ring bearer and flower girl did something cute, as they were supposed to. Everything went the way it was supposed to, which is a relief because so much could have gone wrong.

In other words, the buildup of tension and its release is one of the big ways that a big day (or big story) becomes *big*.

Even better is when the buildup of tension comes from something good that we hope will happen, rather than from fear of something bad. That's an important distinction and applies as much to thrillers as it does to romances. Thus the first task in building a compelling story world is to create hope. The stronger that hope, and the more that we fear it will not be fulfilled, the greater will be the emotional relief when things finally do come out okay.

If we are hoping for something with heart value, so much the better. Making the world a better place for others may inspire our admiration, but what grabs us is a hope for something that we want for ourselves. Think about it: What stirs your hope more? World peace or coaxing a smile from Conchita, the shy young beauty who serves coffee only on Tuesdays at the Barcelona café *Desde el Corazón*? We all have had crushes. We can relate. World peace is an abstraction. It's a hopeless wish. Flirting is human. We can hope to win a smile.

The greatest heart value is love, needless to say, so establishing what and whom your protagonist loves is a useful way to establish heart-touching hope. It's possible to love a place, too, of course. What causes that to happen? When there are good things in a fictional world, we feel good things about it. What kind of things? Good food, fine fellowship, and rightness to everything. Who doesn't want to live in a place like that? Put differently, when your hero is liked, accepted, understood, and supported, a reader's liking for the story's setting grows.

Hostile environments don't make us want to stay. That goes for a story's moral values, as well. We like to be where fairness, justice, and generosity of spirit dwell. To make us love a place, make it a place where goodness reigns—or will again, once your protagonist wins.

EMOTIONAL MASTERY 24:
STORY WORLDS WE DON'T WANT TO LEAVE

- Think about the world of your story. Now think about how your protagonist feels about that world. Is the world basically good and governed by right principles, or is it basically hostile and a place from which you can expect only pain?
- If the former, what or whom is your protagonist's bedrock of goodness? If the latter, how does your protagonist find humor, comfort, or refuge in this hostile place? In a paragraph, write how your protagonist experiences the element of goodness, or write a passage where we see goodness in progress.
- Who is on your protagonist's side? Create a moment in which that care, understanding, and support are shown. How close to the opening of your novel can you place this moment? Page two?
- Whom does your protagonist love? How quickly can you bring this in? If that love is returned, show it. If that love is unrequited, how does your protagonist keep it alive?
- Apart from people, what in your story world is something that your protagonist loves? What warms your protagonist inside? Find a way for us, your readers, to hold, smell, taste, or feel that pleasure, comfort, security, or delight right away.
- Setting aside the plot problem or goal, what does your protagonist hope for? What is human, specific, real, and achievable—something we can visualize? How will we know this drives your protagonist? What's the biggest clue?

Enriching a story world is less a matter of sensory details and more a matter of creating an emotional experience. Drenching your world in chocolate doesn't by itself make it sweet. Rather, it's the spirit of the chocolatier and the way the chocolate affects people that make your place delicious.

GEMS VERSUS NECKLACES: EMOTIONAL LANGUAGE

I love necklaces. No, I'm not a hippie. I'm not a cross-dresser. (Not that there's anything wrong with that.) I just love the many ways in which women make themselves beautiful. A French twist, a bare shoulder, smoky eyes, a pretty necklace. Diamond necklaces are stunning. Not that I see them except in the window at Tiffany's, mind you.

But to be gorgeous a necklace doesn't need to be made of rare gems. Design factors like harmony, balance, proportion, movement, contrast, and emphasis are more important. For instance, harmony is achieved by using similar elements in the composition of the necklace. Wood and clay evoke the earth. Turquoise and silver also are a natural combination, as you can see in jewelry shops all over Santa Fe. Distribute the elements of a necklace evenly and you have balance, but an asymmetrical composition can be as effective, or one in which the visual expectation created on one side of the necklace is offset or reversed on the other. Contrast, such as alternating beads of onyx and opal, is visually interesting if not symbolically intriguing.

In composing a necklace, you can also work with proportion: making pearls larger as they descend toward the necklace's nadir, for example. Complementary color-wheel choices are like variations on a theme. Textural contrasts also catch our eyes. Movement is how a necklace visually directs your gaze, explaining why drop necklaces probably are my favorites.

Ahem.

Now, don't get me wrong. A single diamond solitaire on a woman's left ring finger is a beautiful thing. It's symbolic and emotional. I'm not against rings. But for me an engagement ring and an artfully composed necklace do not compare. One is simple and pure, understood with one look. The other is complex and engaging, demanding that you look again. A bride is a gem, no question, but a married woman is a necklace.

I'm sorry, should I have composed that metaphor the other way around? Never mind. The point is, what's beautiful in necklaces are not gems themselves but the way in which they are arranged. Which brings us to words.

"We live and breathe words," says Cassandra Clare. "Words are wind," says George R.R. Martin. "I am apt to get drunk on words," confesses Madeleine L'Engle. Words. Choosing the right ones preoccupies us. *Luger* is better than *gun*. Is *delicious* or *scrumptious* tastier? Avoid adjectives ending in *-ly*. A word with an Anglo-Saxon root is stronger than a word with a Latin root.

And on we go. Get the right words, and you've got everything right, yes? But here's the thing: The right words are gems, but a word by itself is not a necklace. Words gain their power when we set them in patterns.

In this, poets, debaters, and speechwriters have much to teach us. Academics also have studied the tricks of word patterns and have fancy names for them: alliteration, anaphora, aphorism, assonance, asyndeton, binary opposition, catachresis, chiasmus, epistrophe, euphony, hypallage, inversion, litany, litotes, meiosis, metaphor, metonymy, neologism, nonce words, *occupatio*, onomatopoeia, paradox, parallelism, parataxis, periphrasis, stichomythia, syllepsis, synecdoche, *ubi sunt*, zeugma. You can look up those terms and practice them, or you can keep it simple.

Simple: Use repetition, parallels, or reversals. Be brief. Put strong words at a sentence's end. Compose sentences with symmetry and paragraphs with contrast. (In case you're interested, that last sentence was an example of *zeugma*.)

Or, heck, just make your prose sound good.

I mention all this because when readers read our stories we want them to feel something not small. (Note: Litotes) We want their hearts to ascend mountains. (Note: metaphor + assonance) To do that we cannot just scatter words like tacks or hope the fanciest ones will trigger readers' feelings.

I'm all for gems, but I'm more for necklaces.

Best of all are strong words, especially heart words, strung in shapely patterns. Winston Churchill knew this. When he wanted to stir Britain to war against Germany, he spoke to Parliament in exactly that way:

> We have before us an ordeal of the most grievous kind. We have before us many, many long months of struggle and of suffering. You ask, what is our policy? I will say: It is to wage war, by sea, land and air, with all our might and with all the strength that God can give us; to wage war against a monstrous tyranny, never surpassed in the dark and lamentable catalogue of human crime. That is our policy. You ask, what is our aim? I can answer in one word: victory; victory at all costs, victory in spite of all terror, victory, however long and hard the road may be; for without victory, there is no survival.

Even a hippie would pick up a gun. That's the power of strong words set in elegant patterns. Churchill's call to arms was a diamond necklace.

Pierce Brown's debut science fiction novel, *Red Rising* (2013), a story of a slave rebellion set on Mars, is shot through with lyrical writing. The poetic narration of its sixteen-year-old miner hero, Darrow, a "Red," is intriguingly at odds with his low station. His first-person voice soars like a spiritual at times, though you can see that it's actually built of rhetorical devices familiar to any English literature student. In this passage, Darrow describes his love for his wife, Eo, who is destined to die and thus set him on a path to revolution:

> Since song and dance are in our blood, I suppose it is not surprising that it was in both that I first realized I loved Eo. Not Little Eo. Not as she was. But Eo as she is. She says she loved me before they hanged my father. But it was in a smoky tavern when her rusty hair swirled and her feet moved with the zither and her hips to the drums that my heart forgot a couple of beats. It was not her flips or cartwheels. None of the boastful foolery that so marks the dance of the young. Hers was a graceful, proud movement. Without me, she would not eat. Without her, I would not live.

Anastrophe, antithesis, chiasmus, euphony, hyperbaton, litotes, synecdoche … does it matter what labels we stick on the manipulation of words for effect? Not really. What matters is that we manipulate words for effect.

Reordering syntax is somehow soothing. It lulls us into a receptive state, like the rhythm of poetry or the backbeat of a song. Perhaps it's the result of our mothers' lullabies, sung to us in the crib. Or maybe it's that Shakespeare spoiled us for plain language or that Mark Twain elevated the vernacular into a uniquely American symphony. Whatever the deep reasons, the fact is that elegant manipulation of prose produces an emotional response. It's a free set of tools for the emotional toolbox.

EMOTIONAL MASTERY 25: EMOTIONAL LANGUAGE

- Go anywhere in your manuscript. Pick any piece of description. Use the arrangement of words, not imagery, to mimic what is being described.
- Pick any single piece of dialogue that is long. Make it eloquent, a speech to the nation, a sermon from a mountaintop, folk wisdom, a rant without pause, a whispered confession, a poem.

THE EMOTIONAL CRAFT OF FICTION

- Pick any piece of action. Convey the action not through the action itself but through its effects: wreckage, reactions, instant changes, long-term implications. String them together in a montage about everything around it.
- Fill a memory box, one character's memories of another. Use only images and short-burst sentences. Surprise us with pictures that suggest stories, but don't tell them. Run the memories backward through time, mix them up, or show an evolution. Organize them around a theme like a father's many hats and the occasions on which they were worn. Say everything there is to be said in capsule form, images only.
- Pick anything your protagonist cares about. Write out everything your protagonist *does not feel* about that thing. Make the list long enough to fill a paragraph. In one simple sentence at the end, reverse it all: Tell us what your protagonist *actually does feel* about that thing.
- For a character, create a list that conveys everything that "I am"; e.g., a mom, a nurse, worn knitting needles, nobody's fool, the first line of defense, the court of last resort, a baker's convection oven, a retired seductress, a quick-dry hairstylist, a connoisseur of sweatpants, a Julia Child of the lunchbox.

So, how much poetry do you need in your prose? Let me ask you this: How often do you want readers to feel something significant when they read your novel? Maybe once or twice? I hope not. Why not do more?

CHANGE

Have I been harping on change? There's a reason for that. It's the most powerful way to stir feelings in readers.

Change is a universal experience. We've all gone through it. We cannot avoid it. The passages of life guarantee it. Change is necessary, difficult, wrenching, and individual. When a character in a story changes, we are reminded of the emotional earthquakes of our own lives. We feel for characters, or so we say. We're really feeling for ourselves.

Changes can be small or big, but the biggest effect comes from a turn toward virtue. Change can also be momentary, though, as when a point-of-view character gains insight, makes an intuitive leap, asks the right question, looks at things in a new way, reverses course, or in any other way steps out of the box of our expectations.

Every change, big or small, knocks us off balance, which is good in terms of emotional craft.

In general, what changes in people is belief, behavior, or both. However, the emotional effect of change derives less from the change itself and more from the difficulty in making the change; in resistance to changing. A change that's hard to make has more emotional effect when it happens.

In your fiction, you can amplify the effect of change by squeezing your character between two opposing modes: yin or yang, helpless or reckless, Jeckyll or Hyde, pious or godless, righteous or resigned. It's terrible to be torn. But that's what happens, isn't it? We get stuck. For good reasons, too. Wrong belief and damaging behavior become traps because they are perversely helpful, or at least familiar. Adopting new ways is hard because it requires becoming vulnerable, facing complexity, and accepting ambiguity, as well as feeling alone, unsure, and at risk.

No wonder people resist change and backslide once they achieve it. When achieved, though, change feels good. It's relieving, liberating, and empowering. Change is a turn away from self-pity and toward understanding of self and others. It brings maturity and perspective, and elevates one to a higher consciousness.

Turmoil is let go. Peace is found.

In a real sense, change is the goal of every character and the true ending of every story. Once a protagonist has transformed, the story is effectively over. We are settled inside in a way that plot resolution cannot achieve.

Let's consider an example from current fiction. What greater change can there be than falling in love? It's a before-and-after life event. Life is not the same as before and is never the same after. Two individuals become one. Falling in love is a total transformation of self. Given the ocean of romantic fiction out there, then, it's surprising to me that the actual moment of falling in love is so rarely captured.

An exception is Patti Callahan Henry's folksy, wise, country music song of a novel, *The Perfect Love Song* (2010). Henry's novel is the story of nomadic musician Jimmy Sullivan, who tours with his brother and their band, the Unknown Souls, and whose life changes on a Thanksgiving return to their hometown of Palmetto Pointe, South Carolina. Although Jimmy hoped never to return to the painful memories of his childhood home, his brother is set to propose to his childhood sweetheart and Jimmy has no choice but to tag along. Good thing, because it is his chance to see Charlotte Carrington, with whom he is falling in love and for whom he has written a song—a song that will both celebrate their love and also cause the trouble that nearly destroys it.

On that Thanksgiving Day, the author treats us to a flashback scene of an earlier cookout, when hardened Jimmy softens to Charlotte. As they sit on a back porch together, it plays out like this:

> Now, Charlotte might not be the first person you notice at a party, but by the end of the night, she might be the only one you remember. And this is what happened to Jimmy. Charlotte crossed his mind in the same way as a nice sunset or good meal, a gentle prodding.
>
> Ah, but then months later, when Kara broke up with her fiancé and she and Jack reunited, Kara brought the brothers to her house for a cookout, and Jimmy found himself alone on the back porch

with Charlotte. Mr. Larson had been grilling steaks, and the air was resonant with spices and charcoal, as though the aroma had been embedded in the humidity like rain inside a cloud.

Charlotte stared out over the backyard where they could both see the white-shingled corner of Jimmy's old house. She nodded her head toward the house. "So you lived there when you were little."

"Yep," he said. "I did. I try not to think too much about it. Sometimes when I look at the house it seems like something out of a scrapbook, not really mine at all. We left when I was sixteen."

"I know," she said in this tender voice, almost like she were singing a lullaby to a tired child, and then turned and smiled at him.

Now, when she did this Jimmy felt something shift inside him, but he dismissed the feeling, thinking it was an odd emotion passing over him because of the house and all.

[Charlotte then recalls a story about a time when Jimmy rode his bicycle through the house claiming that the brakes didn't work.]

"Wow," Jimmy said, staring off toward the house. "The bike story. I'd forgotten."

"We do that, don't we?" she asked.

"Do what?"

"Forget the good parts because we are so busy forgetting the bad parts."

And that was the end of that: Jimmy's heart opened wide, as if an earthquake had slipped the tectonic plates of his dismal childhood and moved them aside to let Charlotte's love inside.

Change is hard but that's what we want to read about in fiction. We don't want stories that bog us down; we want stories to release us and allow us to feel that anything is possible. Ordinary citizens can be heroes. Frozen hearts can thaw. Flawed human beings can become just a little bit more perfect.

We want to know that in spite of the difficulty we can all change. We will know that's possible when your characters do.

EMOTIONAL MASTERY 26: MAKING CHANGE

- Think about your protagonist. What is the big change he must go through? Whom will he become? Describe that new self.
- Now work backward. Define the old self, the one we'll meet at the story's beginning. What key behavior will we see? How will we know that your protagonist is happy with her old self? Who validates and encourages that old self? What's good about being stuck?
- What's the first glimmer of the need to change? Find that moment. If it is an observation, that's fine. If possible, turn it into an event. How does the old self fail? What tells your protagonist that there must be a better way?
- Add a mentor character, one who sees the new self in your protagonist before your protagonist does. What can this character do to open a door, point the way, walk the path for a while with your protagonist?
- Add a devil, a character who draws your protagonist back toward her old self. How? How can your protagonist backslide?
- What would show your protagonist that staying the same is insupportable, that change *must* happen? What does your protagonist lose that he cannot get back? What joy remains out of reach?
- What is the most dramatic way in which your protagonist can become his new self? What's the least expected moment, an occasion when the old self ought to reign supreme? When is your protagonist most tempted to go backward? Whom would that slip backward please?
- What triggers the commitment to change? What has become more important to your protagonist than sticking to the old ways? How will we see that? Enact the change symbolically.

SEASONS OF THE SELF

It was Sunday evening. Halfway through Labor Day weekend. We brought our dinner and a bottle of wine to our roof. It's an acre-size terrace atop our Brooklyn apartment building. Around us was a late-summer dusk panorama.

Manhattan was to the west, its skyline turning silhouette, a million lights winking on. We could see the East River bridges with their draped necklaces of lights and blinking red crowns. Planes banked overhead, on final approach to LaGuardia Airport. The sky was stormy, clouds crisscrossing in confusion.

Then, gloriously, a keyhole opened in the sky on the western horizon. Sunset beams burst through, radiating outward, backlighting the clouds in gold. We marveled. We sipped our wine, watched our son skip around, and wished we had brought sweaters. The school year was looming, a summer full of memories fading, a time of fights and finding each other again. Our birthdays were coming up soon.

I slow down rarely, as my wife will tell you. Sitting still and reflecting are luxuries for me. But that evening, I found myself taking measure. At a time when many guys are planning retirement, I felt like I was just getting started. I'd become an elementary school dad. Just ahead were parent friendships and the fight against video game addiction. I was turning over the wardrobe in my closet, buying new suits, yet hanging on to sneakers. I was buying monthly Metrocards, yet also riding a Swiss scooter. I was wondering how to balance work, writing, and family.

At almost sixty I had reached a crossroads that felt more like thirty. That evening was the end of something and the beginning of something else that I could barely define, a phase for which I had no map. Everything was different. My roles were changing. A new book was brewing inside. (You're reading it now.) My professional world, book publishing, was changing, too, as it always is. I was planning to get ahead of the curve, riding a future wave that even now hasn't yet started to swell.

That evening I was becoming a new me—again. I mention this because in many manuscripts the protagonist's sense of self is poorly defined. In even more, a sense of the phases of life is altogether missing. We all have a personal history. So do your characters, and when they transition from one phase to another, we can feel it.

If the transition is there.

How does your protagonist understand his own evolution? Powerful characters are real people. For them to become fully real, you need to create their personal history and then grow it. That doesn't mean writing their biographies or résumés, but rather understanding the stages of self that cannot be captured in a photo album. Growth in self-understanding, an awareness of *who I was* and *who I am becoming now,* is as significant, maybe more so, as anything that a character may do.

Avi's Newberry Medal–winning novel, and multiple-list bestseller, *Crispin: The Cross of Lead*, is the story of a thirteen-year-old fatherless English boy, Crispin, in the year 1377. When his pauper mother dies, Crispin finds himself inexplicably declared a "Wolf's Head," a wanted criminal whom anyone may kill. He escapes, barely, from the village of Stromford, the home of long-absent Lord Furnival, who's off fighting in France, and Furnival's wicked steward, John Aycliffe.

The secret of Crispin's birth will later reveal why he is hunted, but this plot point—easily foreseen—is not what makes Crispin's story compelling. It is Crispin's long inner transformation, which begins with his understanding of his wretched and lowly place in God's scheme:

> Thus our lives never changed, but went round the rolling years beneath the starry vault of distant Heaven. Time was the great millstone, which ground us to dust like kerneled wheat. The Holy Church told us where we were in the alterations of the day, the year, and in our daily toil. Birth and death alone gave distinction to our lives, as we made the journey between the darkness whence we had come to the darkness where we were fated to wait Judgment Day.

Then God's terrible gaze would fall on us and lift us to Heaven's bliss or throw us down to the everlasting flames of Hell.

This was the life we led. It was no doubt the life my forefathers had led, as had men and women since the days of Adam. With all my heart I believed that we would continue to live the same until Archangel Gabriel announced the end of time.

Later, on the run, Crispin must for the first time fend for himself, an independence for which he is not prepared:

I, who had already gone farther from my home than I had ever gone before; I, whose life had become so quickly altered; I, who had never really had to make important choices about anything—now I had to decide everything for myself. The result was that I stayed where I was. In truth, I dreaded going far from the road lest I lose the muddy thread that connected me to the only life I knew. In faith, I did not know how to do otherwise.

On the road, Crispin apprentices himself to a giant traveling juggler, Bear, who adopts him, protects him, and eventually discovers the secret of Crispin's birth. Crispin is Lord Furnival's bastard son, who can enable claims upon the estate when Furnival dies. Crispin has no designs on wealth. When Bear is captured, Crispin wants only to rescue his beloved master. To do this, he must face down his mortal enemy, John Aycliffe:

Furious, he stepped forward and lifted a fist as though to strike me.

In response I held up my hand, using the cross that rested in my palm as a shield.

"I know what happened," I said. "Lord Furnival brought my mother to Stromford. He left her there with me, making you our keeper and granting us only a living death. When Richard du Brey came to Stromford with news that my father had returned to England and was mortally ill, you were charged with killing me. It's you who fear me. You fear I'll become your lord."

He made no response, but his eyes told me that I was right.

Crispin does indeed rescue Bear, who in turn kills John Aycliffe, releases Crispin from his bond, and declares Crispin a freeman. Together they return to the road, where Crispin feels in himself something expressed earlier by the revolutionary John Ball:

> And by the ever-loving God who sits above, my heart was full of more joy than I had ever felt before. I was unfettered, alive to an earth I hardly knew but was eager to explore. What's more, I knew that feeling to be my newfound soul, a soul that lived in freedom.

The change in Crispin's understanding of himself is as radical as can be. Once a timid slave, he becomes empowered and then free. Even in a straightforward young adult adventure novel the seasons of a young self can be measured. Call it growth or turning or anything you like; what makes us magnificently human is not only the changes we go through, but our awareness and celebration of them.

We are what we are, true enough, but we turn to stories to discover what we can become, and how that feels.

EMOTIONAL MASTERY 27: SEASONS OF THE SELF

- What have been the periods, to date, of your protagonist's life? What events began and ended each one? What were the highlight and the low moment of each? What did your protagonist learn (or fail to learn) in each era? Give each era a name.
- How does your protagonist measure time? Create a system. Watch the clock as the novel's events unfold. What hour is it now? And now?
- As your story opens, what phase is your protagonist leaving behind? Detail it. What phase is your protagonist heading toward? List the worrisome questions in his mind.
- At any point in the middle, stop. A change in self is being forced upon your protagonist right now. What makes your protagonist aware of that? What is good about changing? Why does your protagonist want to stay the same?

- At the end, define the new self that your protagonist has become. Detail it. What is familiar about this new self? What is entirely new? What's one thing in your protagonist's world that this new self sees differently? What's one thing that will never change?

NEWTON'S LAW FOR NOVELISTS: CASCADING CHANGE

Do you remember Newton's cradle? It's a desktop toy that consists of five steel balls suspended in a cradle. The steels balls are hung like playground swings but with all five touching each other when at rest. *Click-clack.* When you lift one of the outside balls and let it fall, it transfers its energy through the intermediate three balls, which do not move. The outside ball on the other end, however, swings upward almost exactly as high as you lifted the steel ball on the other end.

In terms of physics, the kinetic energy of the outside ball is transferred through compression of the intermediate balls. It's a shock wave. Energy is lost through the generation of heat, a loss minimized because the balls are made of cold steel. Thus, Newton's law of motion ($F = ma$) is neatly demonstrated. Even if you don't remember all that from high school, you know that Newton figured out something fundamental.

Newton has something to teach novelists. His first law says that when an object is in motion it will continue in motion unless acted upon by another force. Newton's second law says that acceleration of the object is proportional to the force acting on it, and inversely proportional to its mass. The third law states that when the object in motion strikes another object, the other object exerts a force equal to and opposite from the first object's force. It pushes back, as it were.

You can immediately spot the implications for fiction craft, right? Set your protagonist in motion and he'll keep going until he hits an obstacle. What happens at that point depends on how urgently your protagonist is motivated (that is, how forcefully he is moving) and the size of the obstacle (its mass). What interests me the most, though, is how Newton's third law applies. When your protagonist slams into someone else, that second person has no choice but to push back or move.

The type of reaction depends on the size, trajectory, and speed of both your protagonist and the other character. The other character will either stay still, sway, or topple over and perhaps even be flattened as your protagonist rolls through. It depends. The point is, your changing protagonist will always exert a force on others, and vice versa. If that doesn't happen, your story is missing something.

Characters, in a way, carom off each other like snooker balls on the velvet surface of your story. Here then is the application of Newton's law: Protagonists and other characters will always change each other.

They must. Isaac Newton says so, and who's going to argue with him?

Rosie Thomas's *The Illusionists* (2014) is a saga of late Victorian variety theater centered on a cocky, charismatic magician who calls himself Devil Wix. Drawn into his orbit are the novel's many major characters: Eliza Dunlop, an artists' model whose life might easily slide onto the streets; Carlo Boldoni, a magician dwarf; Heinrich Bayer, a builder of automatons and magical apparatus; Jakey, the theater sweeper (later, an actor); and various other characters, including an unscrupulous theater owner, performers, backers, landladies, and more.

All are changed in some way by knowing Devil Wix, who himself is changed only by Eliza. She makes Devil face his past, and eventually marries him. Jakey, the sweeper, is on an upward trajectory, proving himself an able actor, though tormented by his homosexuality and unrequited love for Devil. The most resistant to change is Devil's most important ally, Carlo the dwarf, who is a brilliant performer and the secret behind their greatest illusions. Carlo is also embittered by his stature and further weakened by his illnesses, drink, and envy of Devil.

The varied effect of Devil on others around him surfaces one night after a performance at the theater, when Jakey finds Carlo drunk and wallowing in self-pity. Jakey points out to Carlo that he's better off than some.

> "Better off than some," Carlo repeated. "You mean, I'm not a poor wretch off the spike? I've got a roof over my head, food in my belly and a job of sorts, yes. But I'm still a dwarf. Only in my dreams can I look another man in the eye."
>
> "You're lucky enough. Miss Dunlop's your friend."
>
> "Ah, she can be my friend, Jasper's, Heinrich's, yours even. It's only Devil Wix who'll get a different slice of the cake, sooner or later. Mark my words."
>
> Jakey didn't disagree. He looked forlorn.
>
> Carlo stuck out his jaw. "You sweet on Miss Dunlop? Eh?"
>
> "No. But I think she's kind, as well as pretty. Is that why you don't like Mr. Wix, because of him and her?"
>
> "Eh? You keep your cheeky questions to yourself, boy. I do like him well enough, as it happens. I only can't stand the bloody sight of him, with his grin and his yard-long legs and the damned ooze of his pleasure in being himself." The force of these words seemed to propel Carlo to his feet. He reached an upright position, swayed disastrously, and would have fallen on his face if Jakey had not leapt to catch him in his arms.
>
> "Take care," the boy warned.
>
> Carlo gave a sigh, such a gusty breath it might have stirred the stage curtains. "If I don't, no other living creature will do it for me."
>
> Jakey lost his patience. He shook the dwarf by the shoulders.
>
> "I think you are a mite too sorry for yourself, as well as wasting good effort on being angry about what you can't change. You're

little, but like I said, plenty of people would gladly take your place instead of theirs. See where you are? See all this?"

The boy indicated the proscenium arch and the invisible depth of the theatre with its pillars and gilded box fronts all folded in darkness. The sinister breath in the air had faded and Jakey's gaunt face shone with simple awe. "You and Mr. Wix have got this theatre and your plays and tricks to perform in it, and you get your bread from what ordinary folk think is all pleasure and romance."

Through the gin's maudlin fumes Carlo caught the sense of this rebuke.

"Aye," he said at last. "Aye, maybe. You're a sharp lad, aren't you?"

Devil Wix changes both Carlo and Jake, and while their lives are certainly different because of their association with him, they also change each other, at least briefly. Ultimately, Jakey cannot fix Carlo, nor can Carlo fix Jakey, but in storytelling terms the important thing is that we see each of Thomas's characters affecting the others.

Click-clack. It's the sound of the storyteller's physics, the unavoidable force of human interaction. Newton's law is a law because it's true all the time. Is it true in your manuscript? If not, there's opportunity ahead.

EMOTIONAL MASTERY 28: CASCADING CHANGE

- Look at your current scene. Who are the two principle actors, and how are they at odds? Who wins, who loses? Go deeper. Win or lose, how is your POV character changed inside in this scene? Get that down in words.
- Create a chart. Who are the many characters with whom your protagonist interacts? On the chart, detail how each of those characters affects your protagonist's view of self, the other, problems in the plot, people in general, anything at all, from how to live to something as simple as strategies for Monopoly.
- Pick three of those other characters. Write down how each one is changed, in turn, by encountering your protagonist. Work

out a consequence for each. What will each character do differently because of knowing your protagonist?

- What is one unexpected result of your protagonist's overall journey? How does it ripple outward in the pond, affecting many? Show that.

FEELINGS WITHOUT NAMES

The fleeting beauty of life. The irony of it all. Women! Men! A nameless dread. The exquisite ache of inexpressible love. Is there a greater art than evoking a feeling that has no name? When readers feel those it's magic, a pure human connection, a silent but potent sharing straight from heart to heart. It's like when couples who've known each other forever exchange a look. Who needs words? The look says it all.

Nameless emotional experiences can be dark, too. When we leave the light on, shudder, or feel sick inside at the horror of human cruelty, we are feeling something less specific and yet larger than any feeling we can label. The same goes for sensing the presence and reality of God. It's a feeling for which words like humility, joy, wonder, and awe are inadequate.

Ironically, in fiction there is only one way to understand a feeling with no name: words. How is that supposed to work? How can you evoke something nameless without naming it? Obviously the feeling must be evoked. We are talking not about *telling*, but about *showing* in its highest form.

The least effective way to evoke unstated emotion is with pregnant pauses, "significant" looks, or gestures like shrugs or the dismissive wave of a hand. Overused devices like that have little effect. Snorts, grunts, and exasperated huffs—*Men!*—are similarly pale. By the same token, why bother to evoke feelings in readers that can be readily identified and have accurate names? There's no magic in that. Wonder doesn't arise when readers don't have to wonder.

The art we're seeking is the evocation of tacit feelings that leave the reader helpless to explain and speechlessly certain that they have felt this exact thing themselves. Unique feelings are situation specific. They flare as brightly as fireworks and perish just as quickly. They leave behind a trace, though, of something elusive, an excitement or trepidation too real and yet impossible to convey or re-create.

M.L. Stedman's debut novel, *The Light Between Oceans* (2012), concerns a veteran of the Great War, Tom Sherbourne, who becomes a lighthouse keeper on an island off the Australian coast. His wife, Isabel, and baby, Lucy, who washes up on their shore in a boat, change his life. Before that, early on in the novel, Stedman explains why Tom isolates himself by capturing Tom's complex inner state as he stands high atop his lighthouse:

> For the first time he took in the scale of the new. Hundreds of feet above sea level, he was mesmerized by the drop to the ocean crashing against the cliffs directly below. The water sloshed like white paint, milky-thick, the foam occasionally scraped off long enough to reveal a deep blue undercoat. At the other end of the island, a row of immense boulders created a break against the surf and left the inside as calm as a bath. He had the impression he was hanging from the sky, not rising from the earth. Very slowly, he turned full circle, taking in the nothingness of it all. It seems his lungs could never be large enough to breathe in this much air, his eyes could never see this much space, nor could he hear the full extent of the rolling, roaring ocean. For the briefest moment, he had no edges.
>
> He blinked, and shook his head quickly. He was nearing a vortex, and to pull himself back he paid attention to his heartbeat, felt his feet on the ground and his heels in his boots. He drew himself

up to his full height. He picked a point on the door of the light tower—a hinge that had worked itself loose—and resolved to start with that. Something solid. He must turn to something solid, because if he didn't, who knew where his mind or his soul could blow away to, like a balloon without ballast. That was the only thing that had got him through four years of blood and madness: know exactly where your gun is when you doze for ten minutes in your dugout; always check your gas mask; see that your men have understood their orders to the letter. You don't think ahead in years or months, you think about this hour, and maybe the next. Any thing else is speculation.

He raised the binoculars and scoured the island for more signs of life: he needed to see the goats, the sheep; to count them. Stick to the solid. To the brass fittings which had to be polished, the glass which had to be cleaned—first the outer glass of the lanterns, then the prisms themselves. Getting the oil in, keeping the cogs moving smoothly, topping up the mercury to let the light glide. He gripped each thought like the rung of a ladder by which to haul himself back to the knowable; back to this life.

What, exactly, is Tom feeling? Can you put it into a single word? Probably not, which is the point. He is shell shocked, still traumatized by his time in the trenches. The vast expanse of the ocean around him is too big to take in. He panics. To calm himself he must focus on small immediate details like a loose door hinge.

The passage itself focuses on the ocean, the island's rocky shore, waves, foam, guns, gas masks, battle orders, goats, sheep, brass fittings, oil, glass, prisms. But who is Stedman actually writing about? Tom, and what he feels, which is "the nothingness of it all."

The smaller and more specific the imagery (and there's a lot of it here), the more universal and expansive the unspoken feelings of the point-of-view character. Small visual details turn into big invisible feelings.

EMOTIONAL MASTERY 29:
FEELINGS WITHOUT NAMES

- Find a point in your story at which your protagonist is stuck, stymied, undecided, overwhelmed, or in some other way suffused with inner need without having a means to move ahead.
- Now find something in the vicinity for your protagonist to obsess about. This obsession may be positive or negative or hopefully both. Detail your protagonist's gripes and delights in whatever it is. Observe what is good and bad, beautiful and ugly, meaningful and empty. Be specific. Keep the focus off your protagonist and on this whatever-it-is.
- Finally, be sure that in this moment nothing changes. Leave discord unresolved, messes untidy, beauty overlooked, grumbles unheard, truths ignored, and your protagonist helpless to do anything but notice what others do not. Whatever is, simply is.

What we see from this is that "nameless" feelings do actually have names. It's just that these feelings are 1) conflicting, layered, or complex, and 2) through the observation of something else, not in the description of what cannot be described. Thus, you should detail something solid, something that fronts for the formless. Project what is inchoate onto something external and what was ethereal becomes solid and real.

We've all felt the fleeting beauty of life and will again when your protagonist captures it, in a sense, by talking about something other than the fleeting beauty of life. All feelings have names, actually. The art is in making them seem too complex to quickly label.

CHAPTER SEVEN

The **WRITER'S EMOTIONAL** *Journey*

I meet a lot of writers. It's my job but also my pleasure. Writers are my tribe. They're people undaunted by an art form that's exceedingly difficult to master. They're passionate, insightful, supportive, and smart. Life has meaning and they get that. Some have overcome crippling handicaps and all have sacrificed something to do this thing.

Writers also have amazing personal stories. Sometimes they're downright astonishing. What's puzzling to me is that people with such rich experience to draw upon too often write stories far less dramatic than their own.

How is that possible?

Perhaps caution creeps into the process. Maybe a desire to be taken seriously overwhelms a more natural impulse to be spontaneous and playful. It might also be that writers fear that readers will find dramatic story events to be silly, improbable, or hard to swallow. All evidence is to the contrary, but even so many manuscripts wind up feeling small. Others are the exact opposite: high concepts, enormous plots, and heroic characters that feel anything but genuine.

I believe, though, that there is a deeper reason for the disconnect between writers' lives and the stories they tell. Many fiction writers do not feel worthy of their calling. Writing great stories, they feel, is an experience reserved for those other authors—the native geniuses, the prizewinners, the ones who somehow were born with great talent.

That, I can tell you, is baloney. Great storytellers are smart, intuitive people, but not noticeably more so than most writers I meet. Our greatest storytellers are not born into money; they are not better educated, more tormented, or quicker studies. What they do have that others lack is the confidence that they can pull off improbable stunts on the page and get away with them. Their stories matter, they know that, and consequently they don't have to worry about first printings, reviews, Amazon rankings, or getting interviews on NPR. They know that the art and skill they bring to their stories is responsible for their success. Their reward isn't found in royalty statements, but in their own satisfaction.

Do you think my description fits plenty of unsuccessful writers, too? Maybe so. I meet plenty of that type as well; excellent writers who have become disappointed, detached, cynical, even paranoid believers in timing, chance, and connections. Here's the thing, though. When writers approach their craft that way, it shows. You can sense when fiction is masking cynicism or anger. It may read well, but it feels self-conscious. Its spirit is both defiant and desperate. Cynical writing tries too hard.

The spirit that you bring to your writing desk either infects your pages or enlivens them. Your story events either oppress or excite. Your characters either inspire or leave us indifferent. The difference comes not from your story choices but from you. How you feel inside is how we will feel in reading.

Think of it this way: You know how you can apprehend in an instant what kind of person you are meeting by their clothes, handshake, eye contact, and general demeanor? Your pages are similar. You reveal your inner self right away.

When you write a novel, your characters go on a journey, but so do you. In every scene your characters develop; so do you on the day you write that scene. Your characters have hopes, drive, and nerve, or at least you would like them to. What about you? Do you also have hopes, drive, and nerve?

Believe it, without ever meeting you I'll be able to tell.

In some ways the most important work you do in writing your novel is the work you do on yourself. Everyone knows how difficult writing can be. We've all read the blog posts about writer's block, despair, envy, conflicting roles, crashes, recovery, and ways to stay inspired. That's not what I'm talking about. What I mean is your fundamental outlook, your positive spirit, your embrace of goodness, your faith in humanity. It shows in your generosity, not in supporting your writing friends, but in granting strength to your characters and filling their hearts with expectation.

Some people may read fiction to be frightened, but they never read it to be brought down. They may wish to be challenged, but they don't want to be crushed. They may read for amusement, but they still have heart. They do seek an emotional experience, as I've said, but they also want to come away feeling positive.

This may sound like I'm in favor of pandering to readers, but I'm actually appealing to the good, positive, and inspiring person called *you*. Don't give me easy reading; give me the best of you. When you do, it becomes the best of me, too. Do you believe that it cheapens fiction to make it humane, heart grabbing, filled with goodness? You are not alone in that belief, but I disagree.

What is wrong with uplifting readers? Nothing. You are writing to show us how things are, but aren't you also writing to show us how things can be? Your current novel is not just a report, right? It's a vision. It's a gleeful celebration of what is hard, important, hopeful, and beautiful about life.

In addition to that, your protagonist is all of us. Your secondary characters encompass the range of what it is to be human. Your setting is so lovingly specific that it becomes everywhere. Your voice is that of our age. Your themes matter to us all. Novels that are truly grand, generous, and confident do not come along very often, but why can't such novels be yours every time?

Largeness of spirit may seem like something one is born with, but like story craft, it really comes from practice. It's a choice. In a practical sense, then, how do you get your best self on the page? Let's look at some ways.

POSITIVE SPIRIT

Stories have intentions. They have moods. They send signals to readers that set readers' expectations and influence their orientation to the tale. We could say these signals are sent by the author's voice, but more precisely they come from how protagonists behave, speak, think, and feel on the page.

How does your protagonist see herself? If I were to ask you, you'd probably say that your main character is yearning, challenged, responsible, and active. Am I right? Then why is it that so many protagonists come across instead as suffering, helpless, weak, and lost? If you don't believe me, read my slush pile, or just head to your local bookstore and sample what's on the shelves. Many protagonists are not lit by a spirit of compassion, but are instead infected with woe.

Many stories I read are built on a foundation of pathos. *See how sad things are! Watch my character rise and triumph in spite of that!* While that sounds okay, it is really saying that deep down these authors believe that we are all helpless. The author is saying in effect, *poor me!* The spirit of the author's story is self-pity.

Compassion is different than pathos. Rather than *poor me*, it says *poor you!* It allows plot circumstances to be tragic and personal journeys to be hard, but it doesn't permit defeat to be a pervasive condition of existence. Pathos is rooted in despair. Compassion is rooted in hope. The same story can transmit either feeling to readers. It can burden readers with worry or it can inspire readers to believe.

How characters experience their story in turn determines how readers experience a novel.

What kind of spirit does your protagonist have, positive or negative? When obstacles arise, does your protagonist blame others or himself? Is your protagonist's primary expectation that she will fail to succeed? Is the world around your protagonist one primarily of assistance or of pain? Many protagonists are fundamentally negative, which may create a certain tension but also cannot inspire.

Think about people you know who assume the worst, resist the truth, resent, blame others, beat up themselves, focus on problems, wallow in self-doubt, always compare, agonize, cling, stew, feel bored, expect perfection, take everything personally, let things just happen, and wait for lucky breaks. Are we inspired by such people?

Not so much.

Think about people whose spirit has lifted you. Such people make the best of things, leave the past behind, feel grateful, see their possibilities over their limitations, live in the present, plan ahead, forget fear, smile, communicate, accept setbacks, forgive, earn their keep, take responsibility for their lives, make changes happen, persist, stay interested and even amused by everything that life throws at them. Negative things happen to positive people, but positive people stay positive.

Your characters can be that way, too. Every novelist knows not to make their protagonists whiners, but protagonists must grapple with outward problems and struggle internally. How much? Often too much. I don't mean that protagonists should sail along feeling carefree, but that gloom and negativity is exhausting to read. Medically speaking, negativity isn't recommended if you want to live a happy life. (If you don't believe me, read Dr. Barbara Fredrickson's *Positivity*.) The same is true in stories. Too much negativity kills our involvement, never mind your sales.

Don't get me wrong. I'm not against despair, low points, or crushing plot turns, but I do notice that the characters we remember, and for whom we feel the most, tend to inspire us. They lift us, and the surest way to do that is with a positive spirit. Theirs, yes, but that also means yours.

Ben H. Winters's crime novel *The Last Policeman* (2012), an Edgar Award winner, has a gloomy premise. A giant asteroid called Maia is on a collision course with Earth. In roughly six months, the world will end. Needless to say, people aren't happy. Businesses are going bankrupt. Wage and price controls are in effect. Guns are outlawed. Marijuana is legal. Religious mania and suicide are common. In Concord, New Hampshire, a recently promoted detective named Hank Palace continues to work. The latest suicide in the restroom of what used to be a McDonald's has him suspicious. Back at the station house, he faces the skepticism and indifference of his remaining fellow detectives:

> Culverson is waiting, eyebrows raised expectantly. "Detective Palace?"
>
> "Hard to say, you know? Hey, where do you guys buy your belts?"
>
> "Our belts?" Andreas looks down at his waist, then up, as if it's a trick question. "I wear suspenders."
>
> "Place called Humphrey's," says Culverson. "In Manchester."
>
> "Angela buys my belts," says McGully, who's moved on to the sports section, leaned way back, feet propped up. "The hell are you talking about, Palace?"

"I'm working on this case," I explain, all of them looking at me now. "This body we found this morning, at the McDonald's."

"That was a hanger, I thought," says McGully.

"We're calling it a suspicious death, for now."

"We?" says Culverson, smiles at me appraisingly. Andreas is still at McGully's desk, still staring at the front section of the paper, one hand clapped to his forehead.

"The ligature in this case was a black belt. Fancy. Buckle said 'B&R.'"

"Belknap and Rose," says Culverson. "Wait now, you're working this as a murder? Awfully public place for a murder."

"Belknap and Rose, exactly," I say. "See, because everything else the victim was wearing was nothing to write home about: plain tan suit, off the rack, an old dress shirt with stains at the pits, mismatched socks. And he was wearing a belt, too, a cheap brown belt. But the ligature: real leather, hand stitching."

"Okay," says Culverson. "So he went to B&R and bought himself a fancy belt for the purposes of killing himself."

"There you go," puts in McGully, turns the page.

"Really?" I stand up. "It just seems like, I'm going to hang myself, and I'm a regular guy, I wear suits to work, I probably own a number of belts. Why do I drive the twenty minutes to Manch, to an upscale men's clothing store, to buy a special suicide belt?"

I'm pacing a little now, hunched forward, back and forth in front of the desk, stroking my mustache. "Why not, you know, just use one of my many existing belts?"

"Who knows?" says Culverson.

"And more important," adds McGully, yawning, "who cares?"

"Right," I say, and settle back into my seat, pick up the blue book again. "Of course."

"You're like an alien, Palace. You know that?" says McGully. In one swift motion, he balls up the sports section and bounces it off my head. "You're like from another planet or something."

Does Hank Palace really need to pursue this case? Not really. What does it matter when life on Earth is going to end in six months? Yet something about the circumstances, the belt, bothers him. He needs to know the truth. Is this a kind of madness in a world already gripped by the fear of looming mass extinction? Maybe. Despite having every reason not to care, though, Palace remains devoted to his job. Ben H. Winters doesn't call this positivity, but I do. Truth still matters to Hank Palace, even at the end. Some things are worth fighting for right up to the end.

If that isn't positive thinking, I don't know what is.

EMOTIONAL MASTERY 30: POSITIVITY ON THE PAGE

- Pick a low point for your protagonist. What is happening? How is it a setback? Why does it devastate? What makes this misery different from any other? Describe it. Detail it. Find in it what is unique.
- Add perspective: Why is it good to feel this bad? What can be seen or grasped clearly now that was previously hidden? Whose experience can now be understood? What truth is affirmed?
- What better day can your protagonist see in the distance? In what way does your protagonist express this: "A better day is coming, but that is not this day."
- Add action: What can your protagonist do in response to what has happened? What would be comforting, creative, generous, or large? Do it.
- What kind of mood are you in today? Are you down, discouraged, afraid, anxious, tired, envious, stuck, or lacking confidence? Turn your mood around. Breathe. Meditate. Drink green tea. Go for a run. Use affirmations. Shake it off and become excited, empowered, brave, singular, happy, grateful, curious, and creative.
- Write not just at a safe fifty-five miles per hour but blast off. Break the box. In the scene you're working on, surprise the hell out of yourself.
- In the scene you're working on, what kind of mood is your protagonist in? Does he feel helpless, set upon, oppressed,

avoidant, incapable, or trapped? Turn it around. Show through action or speech that he is capable, challenged, has a plan, has options, can stand strong and affect the outcome.

- In this scene, pause and allow your protagonist to appreciate something cool, neat, beautiful, human, or different.
- In this scene, allow your protagonist to feel that what's happening is good.
- In this scene, find a way for your protagonist to change something.
- If in this scene things go against your protagonist, find a way for your protagonist to suck it up, shrug it off, look ahead, and feel ready.
- If in this scene things go well for your protagonist, find a way for your protagonist to not take it for granted, resolve to do better, reach out to another, and give back.

What did you come up with? Do any of these new elements change the scene's plot purpose or outcome? Do any of these new elements interfere with your protagonist's inner struggles and journey toward wholeness? Does a hint of positivity in your protagonist turn you off?

I will bet not. Positive people are like that. We want to be around them. But, really, whom are we talking about here, your protagonist or you? Pretty obvious, right? Your protagonist can turn a corner in every scene; so can you in every writing session. I'm positive of that.

THE EMOTIONAL MIRROR

Are your characters you? In some ways they must be. After all, they spring from your mind and imagination. They are products of your makeup, experience, wants, fears, and beliefs. The conflicts in which you place them must, by definition, be conflicts that are of concern to you. Their relationships must be ones that feel significant to you. Their emotions are ones you've felt. Their values must be rooted in yours. Their changes must be ones you deem important to go through, as well. Of course they are. Why else would you write about them?

Write about what you know, the old saying goes, and whom do you know better than yourself?

Or do you?

The dictum *know thyself* goes back to the ancient Greeks, and for just as long we've been hiding from ourselves, lying to ourselves, blind to our faults, projecting onto others, repressing, rationalizing, justifying, denying, overconfident, acting, wearing masks, and in any number of other ways avoiding ourselves. No wonder psychotherapy takes years.

Dostoyevsky said, "Lying to ourselves is more deeply ingrained than lying to others." We could chalk this up to being human, but if you are writing fiction, refusing to face yourself has a danger: It means that you are also not fully facing your characters.

Have you ever met a character in a novel who did not feel realistic? Have you met stereotypes or cardboard cutouts? Have you felt that a character's choices were too convenient? Inauthentic characters behave that way because the author needs to keep them in check, contained, safely boxed in. Keeping characters in bounds helps authors avoid feelings of confusion, or being ill at ease, embarrassed, defensive, inadequate, squirmy, or sad.

Real characters take root when you get real with yourself. Be honest and empower yourself, and you will be able to release all the authenticity and power inherent in your fictional people.

How can you do that? The answer is simple: Ask your characters to help.

EMOTIONAL MASTERY 31:
THE EMOTIONAL MIRROR

- After you have written at least some portion of your novel, imagine that you are alone with your protagonist in a quiet, windowless room. You sit facing each other in comfortable chairs. There's plenty of time. The mood is relaxed. You are not defensive. You are thrilled to have this chance to talk with your protagonist, and your protagonist is grateful to talk with you.

- Ask your protagonist to tell you something about yourself that's true. What does she say?
- Ask your protagonist: If you could do anything you wanted to in this story, what would it be? What are you dying to do that I'm not letting you? What's your most wicked impulse? What's your best idea? What would make you happy?
- Ask your protagonist: What are you most afraid that I am going to put you through? How are you afraid you will suffer? What are you afraid you will lose? Are you afraid I will humiliate you? How? What's your worst nightmare? What's the worst way to fail? Whom are you most afraid to let down?
- Ask your protagonist: What am I not seeing about someone else in this story? Who has a secret? Whose motives and objectives aren't what I think? Who is secretly working against you? Who, by contrast, is better than they appear? What does any other character want to do that they're not getting a chance to do now?
- Ask your protagonist: What do you want to say out loud that you haven't said? Whom do you want to tell off? To whom do you want to confess, I love you? Whom do you want to hurt? Whom do you want to seduce, or be seduced by? Whom do you want to help and cannot help now? Whom do you want to forgive?
- Ask your protagonist: What's this story really about—to you? What am I not seeing? What message have I missed?

Fiction is an emotional mirror, a mirror that reflects you. There's much you can learn about yourself through writing, and even more that your characters can reveal to you. Their freedom to speak is your freedom to grow. Characters can help you see what you've been avoiding and reveal to you the unused potential in your story. Nice of them, isn't it?

LOVE THY NEIGHBOR: DECENCY AND GOODNESS

The signals sent to readers come not only through your characters, but also through your novel's world. We can experience that world the way that your characters do, a technique I've talked about in *Writing 21st Century Fiction*, but we can also experience it the way that anyone and everyone would. It requires looking at your setting as a community to be felt and a place to be visualized.

How do you see the world of your story? Warm and embracing? Icy and hostile? What kind of people live there? Is everyone the same? Certainly not, yet that is how authors' worlds feel in an awful lot of fiction. We sense that in protagonists' isolation. Authority is malign, families are toxic, friends and sidekicks skew generic and ultimately can't help. Is that how your own real world seems to you? Some days, no doubt, but probably deep down you feel as I do: People are basically good.

I'll give you an example.

Hurricane Sandy hit New York City hard. Downtown in the West Village, where we lived, we watched the storm with our fingertips on our windows, the glass ballooning inward. We saw the Hudson River rise. Piers disappeared. The West Side Highway became a river. Our block-long apartment building became an ocean liner aground in a shallow sea.

The blackout that followed was, for us, seven nights long. The first night, our neighbors converged in our pitch-black hallway with flashlights and candles. Where were the emergency lights? Fire alarm? (We later learned we were supposed to evacuate.) We discussed what to do. Stick it out? Head out of town? How? The subways, railroads, airports, bridges, and tunnels were all closed. Cars in the parking lot across the street were under water.

In subsequent days, we joined the army of downtown refugees heading uptown into the power zone north of 26th Street for cell phone charging, hot meals, and coffee. You could tell who our neighbors were. They were warmly dressed, pushing strollers, looking like they needed a shower.

And they talked. People who ordinarily would keep eyes averted on the sidewalks and subways were eager to share stories. *Are you okay? Do you have water? What have you heard? Hi, I'm Don. This is my wife, Lisa, and our son, Abi. Nice to meet you. Where do you live? Which school are your kids in?*

I collected business cards and handed out mine. After a week, the power came back and I never heard from most of those people again, but for a little while we were a community. New York City is like that in a crisis. It was the same after 9/11. The city shut down but people pulled together. After Hurricane Sandy I thought about what had happened. We had gone through a big problem together. We'd lived a story. And how did people behave during that story? Did they shun each other?

No, just the opposite. In a way it was excellent to live in the dark. I discovered again how good people can be.

So what has that to do with manuscripts? It's not often that I read about a fictional place and wish I lived there. But once in a while those magical places appear on the page and welcome me. It's a combination of the place and the people. There's a warmth, a comfort, a sense that whatever the conflict there's an innate goodness to the folks there.

I feel at home.

How does such a place come about on the page? Even in a dystopia there's room for goodness, a safe corner for your readers— sorry, I mean your characters. Indeed the darker the times, the more hostile the environment, the more people's innate goodness shines. Small towns can be small-minded, but they can also be warm and supportive communities. It's a factor of the people who live there.

John Grisham's autobiographical novel *A Painted House* (2001) is set in Arkansas cotton country in 1952. It's a coming-of-age story about seven-year-old Luke Chandler, whose family, come harvest time, wants to bring in the cotton and pay off their debts. For this they must hire migrant Mexican workers and the "hill people," whites even poorer than the Chandlers are. The differences in the cotton country social strata are stark, and lead to romance and death reminiscent of John Steinbeck's *Of Mice and Men* (1937) and explored again in Robert Goolrick's *Heading Out to Wonderful* (2012), among other novels.

Despite its tragic plot turns, Grisham's novel is soaked in the goodness of this country community. The nostalgic glow is not only made up of biscuit breakfasts, Cardinals games on the porch radio, and the Sears Roebuck catalog; it's also the people of the town, who all know each other well. As the novel opens, Luke is on his way to town with his slow-driving and beloved grandfather, Pappy, to see about hiring workers. Luke has a Tootsie Roll on his mind, his go-to-town treat.

> I waited on the sidewalk until my grandfather nodded in the direction of the store. That was my cue to go inside and purchase a Tootsie Roll, on credit. It only cost a penny, but it was not a foregone conclusion that I would get one every trip to town. Occasionally, he wouldn't nod, but I would enter the store anyway and loiter around the cash register long enough for Pearl to sneak me one, which always came with strict instructions not to tell my grandfather. She was afraid of him. Eli Chandler was a poor man, but he was intensely proud. He would starve to death before he took free food, which, on his list, included Tootsie Rolls. He would've beaten me with a stick if he knew I had accepted a piece of candy, so Pearl Watson had no trouble swearing me to secrecy.
>
> But this time I got the nod. As always, Pearl was dusting the counter when I entered and gave her a stiff hug. Then I grabbed a Tootsie Roll from the jar next to the cash register. I signed the charge slip with great flair, and Pearl inspected my penmanship. "It's getting better, Luke," she said.

"Not bad for a seven-year-old," I said. Because of my mother, I had been practicing my name in cursive writing for two years.

[Pearl asks where Luke's grandfather is. He's in The Tea Shoppe, checking on the Mexicans.]

Pearl grinned whenever I called my grandfather by his first name. She was about to ask me a question when the small bell clanged as the door opened and closed. A genuine Mexican walked in, alone and timid, as they all seemed to be at first. Pearl nodded politely at the new customer.

I shouted, "Buenos días, señor!"

The Mexican grinned and said sheepishly, "Buenos días," before disappearing into the back of the store.

"They're good people," Pearl said under her breath, as if the Mexican spoke English and might be offended by something nice she said. I bit into my Tootsie Roll and chewed it slowly while rewrapping and pocketing the other half.

The goodness and decency of the folks in Luke's community (well, most of them), is evident not just because Pearl sneaks Luke forbidden Tootsie Rolls, but because she welcomes a Mexican migrant worker into her shop. Grisham spent his first seven years at his grandfather's cotton farm, so perhaps his memories of the area are a bit rosier than the reality actually was. Still, he anchors his fictional place, and us, in a fundamental decorum and goodwill that lets us know that the world of this story is a safe place, even if Luke is destined to see its harsher side and grow up.

EMOTIONAL MASTERY 32: DECENCY AND GOODNESS

- What's the nicest thing about people in the time and place you're writing about? Find a way for us to experience that early in your story.
- Who in your cast is generous, bighearted, empathetic, insightful, or wise? Make sure we meet that character early.

- Toward the beginning of your story, let someone reach out to help someone else. If possible, involve food.
- In the world of your story, what's the equivalent of a Sunday picnic, backyard barbeque, school dance, country fair, town meeting, Fourth of July parade, old-time diner, or corner bar? Set a scene there.
- What are the highest values in the world of your story? What's the most dramatic way in which they can be enacted? Go ahead, you know what to do.

Once in a great while I read a manuscript where everyone is too nice. Far more commonly I slog through stories in which I meet hardly anyone nice at all. Warming up your story's world is not dangerous. The worst that will happen is that it will seem more real. Why? Because it captures the inherent goodness of human beings.

Add some light and your readers will be less afraid of the dark. Even better, they'll be glad they came.

MAGNANIMOUS

Do you have a game face? Is your personality different at your desk, on a date, and in the stands at the ballpark? Are you hard charging at work but relaxed on weekends? Are you foul-mouthed in the privacy of your car but eloquent when making a wedding toast? Can you be patient with children but not with fools? When are you at your worst? When are you at your best?

You are different depending on the day, right? Maybe even the hour? Who isn't? There are times when you are great to be around. There are other times when the world should quietly tiptoe backward from you, palms raised. You no doubt feel that way about others, too. There's the friend who's a riot on one drink but blistering to be around after three. In your family there's the complainer and the saint. There are colleagues who are great company and others who, at six, you're happy to leave behind.

Generally speaking, we choose company that is pleasant. People who are warm, open, curious, compassionate, and interesting are good to be around. We gravitate to people like ourselves, who share our outlooks, interests, and values. It's nice to spend time with pleasant people, isn't it?

So, question: What kind of person are you asking your readers to spend four hundred or more pages with? What sort of company are you providing for your readers? I don't mean just the temperament of your protagonist, but your own. What sort of spirit are you bringing to your fiction? What vibe are you putting out on your pages? In manuscripts, I meet many protagonists who are sour, snarky, bemused, self-pitying, singly focused, disconnected, or, frankly, just plain dull.

This would seem to fit the framework that says protagonists should be yearning, obsessed, suffering, isolated, and in need of change. Sure, I get that, but spending time with such people can be a drag. Their spirit is negative. Many would say "redemptive," since everything comes out great at the end, but endings are far off. We still have a long, miserable middle to endure.

The solution isn't necessarily creating characters who are relentlessly chipper and nothing but fun, though that might be a relief. Yearning, need, struggle, and change are essential to good story, yet all of that can be accomplished in a spirit that invites us in more than makes us run screaming.

The difference lies in how you, the author, feel about your characters, the story world, and everything in general. You are what you eat, right? In the same way, what you write is you. So what are you serving up?

What is your best self? I will bet that your best self is generous, curious, compassionate, understanding, insightful, discerning, and large. You are humorous, have an eye for irony, and rue human nature even while you are tolerant of it. You are far seeing, wise, and you grasp truths that others do not see but should. You've learned from experience and value days that throw you curves. You see life not as a problem to solve or as something to survive, but as a feast for the senses and good material for fiction. You love life and shape your experience in service of a greater good.

For you, story is not just a plot to wrestle to the ground or a journey to take, but a celebration of human endurance, a forgiveness of our sins, a bountiful grace to bestow, a freedom to roam, a greathearted kindness, and a high-minded call to our better natures. You tell stories with purpose but without judgment. You trust yourself to create, your characters to act in ways beyond the ordinary, and your readers to bring stout hearts to situations that are tough and troublesome.

In a word, you are magnanimous. You are the best our human race has to offer. I know this because you write.

But I ask you, is that spirit truly shining through on every page? Let's face it: Some writing days are a dog. Sometimes it's a struggle to get through a page. That shows. The process of writing a novel is long and exhausting. We can feel that in the read. When you're cranky, so is your novel. When you shine, your novel does, too. So why not let yourself shine, both in life and on the page?

EMOTIONAL MASTERY 33:
MAGNANIMOUS WRITING

- Stop at any point in the story. What's funny here? What's ironic? What's peculiar, crazy, wrong, and out of bounds? Why is that somehow just perfect right now?
- Stop at a point of pain. What's beautiful despite the darkness? For what can your POV character be grateful? If this had to happen, what's the saving grace?
- Think about your story world. What's wonderful about it? What's the greatest good? What should be shared? What would we love about it even more if we knew?

- Think about your protagonist. Find one way to set this character free. What's a gift you can give your protagonist? In what unexpected way can he be fulfilled? What dream experience could come true?
- Think about a time of pressure. What is excellent about this challenge? What's cool, awesome, and exciting about being in this situation? How can your protagonist be creative? How can your protagonist exceed her own expectations, and even your own?
- Pick a secondary character. What potential does your protagonist see in this person that others miss? What façade can your protagonist see through? What flaw is forgivable? What strength can be admired?
- Who in the story can rise above a situation? Who can forgive when forgiveness isn't earned? Who is high who can show humility? Who is low who can muster dignity? Who can open their home? Who can impose tough love? Who can sacrifice? Who can inspire? Who can admit wrong? Who can show love when damnation is deserved?
- Pick any page in your manuscript. What's happening? Who in this scene can act more noble, strong, just, fine, generous, loyal, or principled?
- Pick another page. What is unseen, surprising, symbolic? What demonstrates a principle or proves a point? Who gets that?
- Pick another page. What do you enjoy about anyone on this page or anything that's happening? Find a way for your feeling to shine through. How would you sum it up? Who on the page can think, say, or show what's in your own mind?

Magnanimous is a quality but also a practice. It's something to embrace every writing day and on every page. When you do, not only will readers be caught by your spirit and transformed, but they will forget that it's happening and attribute the buoyancy they feel to the story they're reading.

Actually, it's coming from you. So, what is your best self and how is that spirit shining in the scene you're working on right now? Go on, be generous. You've got heart to spare. Spread it around. When your spirit is large, your stories can be, too. So can the world that we all share.

THE CURRENT

What is it about a novel that sweeps us up into its world? What carries us along even when the imperatives of plot are on hold or absent? What makes us ache for something without knowing what it is? What makes us impatient for a story's resolution while also hoping the tale goes on forever? What is it that causes us to feel that a story has touched our souls? It's not plot, scene dynamics, or microtension. It's not the inner journey. It's not setting, voice, or theme, even though those things undeniably affect us. What I'm talking about is a deeper, seemingly mystical force that engages readers in a way they can't explain and holds them rapt. It's nothing overtly stated in your pages.

That irresistible, invisible current is a feeling, one that readers can only sense and for which they do not have a name. What causes them to experience this feeling is not so much anything that you put into your story as it is the spirit that underlies it, a spirit that you bring.

Hope.

Hope is not something easily contained in one story moment. It's a difficult feeling to deliberately stir in readers, and one that does not lead characters into action. In fact, it's not really part of the story at all. Rather, it's a longing, an ache, for something unnamed and unobtainable that you cause readers to believe is both real and possible.

Readers experience hope as anticipation, but it is often mistaken for something else. For example, consider a classic low-grade horror movie scene. You know the one. It's the scene in which a teenaged boy and girl are walking up to a derelict cabin in the woods at night. The boy is saying, "Come on, Susie, let's go inside!" Susie says, "Oh, I don't know, Johnny. That place looks creepy. Can't we go back to town?"

Johnny talks Susie into going inside, at which point we know these two are too stupid to live and richly deserve what will be done to them by the monster in the leather mask. It's the expectation of the gore to come that causes us anxiety, right? Well, maybe. But there's another emotional force at work, one that is as strong as or stronger than our fear. What's triggering our feelings isn't only Johnny saying, "Let's go inside!" It's Susie saying, "Can't we go back to town?" Susie is the voice of hope. We hope, just for a second, that Johnny is not as stupid as he looks, that he'll make a good decision, and that he'll save Susie from torture and evisceration. Our feeling is partly "Look out!" but just as much it's "Please, please don't die!" (Unless the movie is really bad.)

An absence of hope explains some puzzles about fiction, for instance, why thriller writers can sometimes pile on more and more danger, raise the stakes higher and higher, yet give us barely an ounce more thrill. It explains why beautifully rendered literary fiction can feel ice cold, even when its endings are redemptive. It's why certain dark mysteries depress us while others nearly identical in plot have us cheering.

Hope is the current running through fiction that we love. So what is it that we hope for? Happy endings? Certainly, but that's only part of it. Hope can be found in every dimension of the stories we adore.

Take a story's world. Settings can convey hope. Does that sound impossible? It's not. Hope arises when characters are presented with a destiny. A story world that gives us hope is also a place where peace is always a possibility. In such places we find ourselves energized by expectation.

When hope brims in novels it's found in characters who look inward with interest and regard others with curiosity. It's experienced through a need not to avoid what's bad, but to seek what's good. It's felt not in a series of setbacks, but in a rising curve of yearning.

It's evident in characters we love because their hearts are more generous than ours can ever be. When we want stories to go on forever, they're lifting up our eyes. In stories full of hope, we care about a character's soul as much as their safety. Authors with hope are overcome by love.

If hope must come through words, then what words? When there's no technique to apply, what tools do you use? Luckily, the tool you need is one you already have: It's you, since you are the embodiment of hope. All you need do is let it flow into your characters, their outlook, and their world.

Paradoxically, or perhaps with perfect logic, stories that inspire us with hope can sometimes begin with characters in situations of utter hopelessness. Think *Les Miserables* by Victor Hugo.

Characters can at first be wretched, too, which makes their later redemption all the more amazing and inspiring. Why should we feel anxious for someone who is already good at heart and whose life is trouble-free? We don't, or at least we won't, until some heart-wrenching plot problem arrives. A character who is a miserable human being begs for a beautiful change even before a single thing has happened; however, our care for such a wretch does not come automatically. We need signs that such a character is worth redemption and that redemption will, eventually, arrive.

Swedish author Fredrik Backman's *A Man Called Ove* (2014) is the story of a curmudgeon named Ove, a fifty-nine-year-old grump to beat all grumps. Fortunately, he is also humorous, even while he is acidic in outlook, grim in demeanor, unpalatable, and utterly dark. Ove is not happy-go-lucky. Left empty by the death of his wife, he repeatedly attempts suicide, though each try is interrupted by the arrival of people who need his help or want to be nice to him. Attempting to be hit by a train, he instead manages to save people stuck on the tracks. He has plenty of reason to be sour.

Ove patrols the parking lot of his apartment complex. He is befriended by a cat and picks up a number of unlikely allies: a pregnant Iranian immigrant neighbor and her husband, a yuppie, a journalist, and a trio of lost or conflicted young men, one drifting, another flamboyantly gay, and another overweight. In flashback chapters, Ove remembers his hard childhood and relationship with his dead wife, Sonja, and the accident that took her legs. Ove also is drawn into the situation of two former friends, Rune and Anita, to whom Ove has not spoken in decades. Rune and Anita are now struggling with Rune's advancing Alzheimer's disease. When plans are made to move Rune to a care facility, Ove is angered enough to help, despite his long estrangement from the couple.

A Man Called Ove is a novel brimming with hope, an odd thing to say when its protagonist is so crabby. What causes us to feel that hope? Before it is Ove himself, it's the actions of others. Take the cat. It's found in the snow outside Ove's apartment. His pregnant neighbor insists Ove take it in and nurse it to health. (The neighbors can't, as they are allergic.) Ove is reluctant, to say the least, but he does save the cat. One snowy day he brings the cat along with him as he brings flowers to his wife's grave:

> "I've brought some flowers with me," he mumbles. "Pink. Which you like. They say they die in the frost but they only tell you that to trick you into buying the more expensive ones."
>
> The cat sinks down on its behind in the snow. Ove gives it a sullen look, then refocuses on the gravestone.
>
> "Right, right ... This is the Cat Annoyance. It's living with us now. Almost froze to death outside our house."
>
> The cat gives Ove an offended look. Ove clears his throat.
>
> "He looked like that when he came," he clarifies, a sudden defensive knot in his voice. Then, with a nod at the gravestone:
>
> "So it wasn't me who broke him. He was already broken," he adds to Sonja.
>
> Both the gravestone and the cat wait in silence beside him. Ove stares at his shoes for a moment. Grunts. Sinks onto his knees in the snow and brushes a bit more snow off the stone. Carefully lays his hand on it.

"I miss you," he whispers.

There's a quick gleam in the corner of Ove's eye. He feels something soft against his arm. It takes a few seconds before he realizes that the cat is gently resting its head in the palm of his hand.

Ove does not reach out to the cat; the cat reaches out to him. It's the selflessness of others that gets to us; better still when it's a cat or dog! Other humans can inspire us to hope as well, of course, and such a moment occurs in another novel with a protagonist whose life is miserable: Australian author Bryce Courtenay's *The Power of One* (1989), a novel set in South Africa during the 1930s and 1940s. It concerns an English-speaking boy, Peekay, who is tormented in a boarding school where the other boys speak Afrikaans. They call him *Piskop* (piss-head), torture him, urinate on him, and make him eat feces. The head boy, called The Judge, is a Nazi sympathizer.

Peekay is assisted by a number of adults who teach him principles that will eventually guide his life. One of these adults is a man named Hoppie Groenwald, a rail worker whom Peekay meets on his way to spend a summer with his grandfather in the town of Barberton. Hoppie is a boxer who sees potential in Peekay and teaches him the sport. Hoppie is a welterweight whose strategy is to be smarter than his opponents. "First with your head, then with the heart" is his maxim, which Peekay takes in. To demonstrate, Hoppie arranges a match against a boxer twice his weight known as Jackhammer Smit. The match is not easy and goes thirteen rounds, during which Hoppie is nearly done in, but he sticks to his strategy of targeting his opponent's eyes:

> Hoppie landed a straight left into Jackhammer's face, starting his nose bleeding again. He followed this with several more blows to the head but his punches lacked strength. Jackhammer, his pride keeping him on his feet, managed to get Hoppie into a clinch, in an attempt to sap what strength the smaller man had left. When the referee shouted at the two men to break, Jackhammer pushed at Hoppie and at the same time hit him with a round-arm blow to

the head that carried absolutely no authority as a punch. To our consternation and the tremendous surprise of the miners, Hoppie went down. He rose instantly to one knee, his right hand on the deck to steady him. Jackhammer, sensing from the roar of the crowd that his opponent was down, dropped his gloves and moved forward. Through his bloodied fog he may not have seen the punch coming at him. The left from Hoppie came all the way from the deck with the full weight of his body to drive the blow straight to the point of Jackhammer Smit's jaw. The giant crashed unconscious to the canvas.

"Timber!" Big Hattie screamed as the crowd went berserk. I had just witnessed the final move in a perfectly wrought plan where small defeats big. First with the head and then with the heart. To the very end Hoppie had been thinking. I had learned the most important rule in winning ... keep thinking.

...

In my excitement I was jumping up and down and yelling my head off. It was the greatest moment of my life. I had hope. I had witnessed small triumph over big. I was not powerless.

Hoppie wins the match, but it is Peekay who is empowered. We in turn are inspired by the selfless act of a rail worker to show a boy that small and smart can triumph. Hoppie is a boxer, but his lesson is an act of kindness, and it is the kindness of strangers that stirs in us hope.

EMOTIONAL MASTERY 34: INFUSING HOPE

- Is your story meant to evoke fear? In addition to making circumstances worse, find three ways to raise the hope that the worst won't happen, then an additional three ways to make survival matter more. Make those reasons personal.
- Is your story meant to be romantic? In addition to erecting obstacles to keep two people apart, find three ways to make it matter even more that they join together. Make those reasons personal.

THE EMOTIONAL CRAFT OF FICTION

- Is your story meant to uphold a principle, such as justice? What does your protagonist hope for that cannot be obtained by any means available to him? Find three ways to elevate that hope over the plot goal.
- Is your story one of journey, healing, or seeking wholeness? Find three new ways to manifest the warmth that remains in a wounded heart.
- Whatever your type of story, find people in your story who can do the following: deliver a gift, provide insight into someone else, turn a corner, forgive the unforgivable, humble themselves, see ahead, know the exact right thing to say, back off, be overjoyed, do a favor, change a life, alter a destiny, find the humor, see the irony, grasp the greater meaning, or die with grace. Whatever you find, add it.

When fiction feels effortless it is in part because tremendous talent and skill have been brought to bear. It is perhaps also because of multiple drafts, beta readers, and editorial assistance. It might be that a certain security comes with writing a series, or with experience. Word craft helps, too, but none of that is the same thing as giving a novel heart.

Heart is a quality inherent not in a manuscript but in its author. It is not a skill but a spirit. Spirit may seem mystical, but it's not an accident. It can be cultivated and practiced. Every day it can seep into the story choices you make. The spirit you bring is the spirit we'll feel as we read, and of all the feelings you can excite in your readers the most gripping and beautiful is the spirit of hope.

CONCLUSION

You can read a novel or you can experience it. Experiencing it means feeling immersed, rapt, caught up in the spell of the story, as if what's happening to the characters is happening to you. It's not, of course. What you're experiencing is actually happening inside your own mind and heart.

To achieve that effect on readers requires that you, the author, be immersed, rapt, caught up, and settled down in characters' emotional lives as if they are your own. It demands being open, authentic, free of fear, unrestrained by genre requirements or the expectations of fans, critics, the publishing industry, or your own literary heritage and tribe. It calls for you to take positions and declare truths.

What is truth? In our postmodern age, we may scoff at absolutes, but fiction doesn't care about that. Fiction persuades. As in court, tell the best story and the judge and jury are likely to take your side. Reach readers' hearts and they'll not only immerse in your story, but believe what it says.

True novelists have an instinct for conflict. They see surprises hidden all around. Writers love to watch people, but that action is not idle and passive; writers peer into those passersby. They wonder how strangers became the people that they are. Writers exploit their own family weirdness without shame. Scenarios spin and worlds build in their minds. They trust their own instincts to tell them what is *right* in a story. They know when they're faking it and aren't afraid to start over.

How does one develop the instincts, eyes, and heart of a novelist? Story means something different to every fiction writer. Personality, preferences, politics, and gender are factors. Female authors can view female characters as wounded, their inner journeys taking them toward healing and strength. Male authors can go the opposite way, creating male characters full of hubris. Such protagonists need not to heal, but to find humility; need not to gain power, but to learn power's limits.

No set of characters or idea for story is wrong; they're simply less effective when they're not entirely one's own. Most of all, true novelists do not feel a need to apologize for what they're doing. Virginia Woolf and Ernest Hemingway had their problems, but they did not write blog posts about staying inspired, pitching anxiety, rejection fears, or publication jitters. They wrote in the confidence that their stories were necessary, a calling, and important to write even if they were not welcomed with accolades.

Austen, Dickens, Hardy, James, Wharton, Fitzgerald, Hemingway, Hammett, Dreiser, Doctorow, Heller, Powell, Pynchon, and many others tackled their times in a deliberate way. Verne, Huxley, Tolkien, Golding, Bradbury, Burgess, Dick, Vonnegut, Atwood, King, and many others turned speculation and fantasy into concrete statements about human nature. Lawrence, McCullers, Tarkington, Conrad, Wright, Penn Warren, Jones, Fowles, Irving, McCarthy, and others have taken personal experience and made it universal—fiction both of its time and yet timeless.

Fiction doesn't need to beg for its place in our culture. It doesn't have to whine about its importance. It doesn't have to be literary in intent to elevate us, either. Historical fiction, sagas, science fiction, crime, coming of age, and other story types have all served a higher purpose than simple entertainment.

Fiction can do things that no other art form can. It engages the imagination on a deeper level, stirs minds and hearts, and brings about change in a way that few other art forms can manage. Why, then, is there a pervasive anguish in the community? Why do fiction writers fear that no one reads anymore? Why do they wring their hands over discoverability? Lack of confidence freezes fingers on keyboards and shows in the timidity and low impact of the pages we read. That is ridiculous.

It is time for all novelists to own the mandate, get beyond their fears, and write with force. What is holding them back? What is holding *you* back? The ultimate in emotional craft is nothing more than trusting your own feelings. Having faith. Confidence. I don't mean just the faith that you will be published. I don't mean only the confidence that you can master the craft. No, I mean faith in your mandate as a storyteller and your fearless surrender to the heroes and monsters inside you.

Protagonists and antagonists are fanatics. So are you. Is that scary? Sure, but own that side of yourself and you are less likely to shut it down. I mean, who wants to admit, *I could kill*? Who wants to confess crazy thoughts and tell the truth about irrational love? Who is ready to remove a mask and make the messy inner self plain for all to see? Then again, why not? That is what storytellers do.

All of us have done wrong. We all can inflict harm, be careless, believe without evidence, rant, and embark on quixotic crusades. We all love without reason and give passes to abhorrent behavior. We are driven by instinct and choose on impulse. Our decisions make no sense economically or morally. Science has proven that we are irrational on pretty much every level.

At the same time, we are grounded in our sense of decency, justice, and what is right. We are flawed, but we are also good. In other words, we have everything we need to tell stories full of human authenticity and emotional truth. There is nothing at all to hold us back. Nothing at all. Nothing more is needed. Right now, this minute, you have the instinct, eyes, and heart of a true novelist.

You do. What you may not have is belief. So I'm here to tell you: believe. You don't need more years, manuscripts, acceptance, likes, stars, movie deals, money, or anything else material to be a true novelist. You are that novelist already because you are human. If you need more practice, polish, craft, coffee, time, or a bigger team in your corner, don't worry. Keep going and those things will come. What you need before and beyond all of that is faith. Craft tools, process, story ideas, and support are important, no question, but your essential humanity and goodness matters more.

Emotional craft is a skill set, don't get me wrong, and I hope this book has helped you sharpen those skills. There is one thing I cannot teach you, though, and that is how to experience this great human experiment of ours. Your unique way of feeling about everything is yours alone, as it should be. If it were exactly the same as mine, then I wouldn't need to read your fiction. But it isn't, and I do. I need to read your stories. And I will when you cause me to feel them in the ways we've discussed.

Do you trust your feelings? Do you believe that they are worthy? Are you able to stop worrying about plot and start embracing the emotional experience that will authentically connect you to your characters, and me to them? Are you open? Are you relaxed? Are you ready? Getting out of your comfort zone is no more difficult than getting into what you feel. Not what you think your characters should feel, I mean, but the vast palette of unexpected, conflicting, troublesome, inspiring, beautiful, mean, and altogether human emotions that shake us and amaze us every day of our lives.

Writing a novel is itself an emotional journey akin to falling in love, living together, hating each other, separating, reconciling, gaining perspective, accepting each other, and finally finding deep and abiding love. Writing fiction is like living. By the same token, one must live fully and generously to write well. The emotional craft of fiction is a set of tools, yes, but more than anything it's an instrument beyond the range of any book: the gracious gift of your own loving heart.

The EMOTIONAL MASTERY Checklist

ACKNOWLEDGMENTS

From *Crispin: The Cross of Lead* by Avi, copyright © 2002 by Avi, published by Hyperion Books for Children.

From *A Man Called Ove* by Fredrick Backman, copyright © 2012 by Fredrik Backman, translation copyright © 2014 by Henning Koch, published by Atria Books, an imprint of Simon & Schuster, Inc.

From *The Double Bind* by Chris Bohjalian, copyright © 2007 by Chris Bohjalian, published by Shaye Areheart Books, an imprint of the Crown Publishing Group, a division of Random House, Inc.

From *Fahrenheit 451* by Ray Bradbury, copyright © 1953 by Ray Bradbury, renewed 1981 by Ray Bradbury, published in the United States by Del Rey Books, an imprint of The Random House Publishing Group, a division of Random House, Inc.

From *Red Rising* by Pierce Brown, copyright © 2013 by Pierce Brown, published by Del Rey, an imprint of Random House, a division of Random House LLC, a Penguin Random House Company, New York.

From *The Girl with All the Gifts* by M.R. Carey, copyright © 2014 by Mike Carey, published by Orbit, a division of Hachette Book Group, Inc.

From *The Hunger Games* by Suzanne Collins, copyright 2008 by Suzanne Collins, published by Scholastic, Inc.

From *The Power of One* by Bryce Courtenay, copyright © 1989 by Bryce Courtenay, A Ballantine Book, published by The Random House Publishing Group.

From *All The Light We Cannot See* by Anthony Doerr, copyright © 2014 by Anthony Doerr, published by Scribner, a division of Simon & Schuster, Inc.

From *My Cousin Rachel* by Daphne du Maurier, copyright © 1951 by The Estate of Daphne du Maurier, published by Virago Press, an imprint of Time Warner Books UK.

From *The Walk* by Richard Paul Evans, copyright © 2010 by Richard Paul Evans, published by Simon & Schuster, Inc.

From *Those Who Leave and Those Who Stay* by Elena Ferrante (translated from the Italian by Anne Goldstein), copyright © 2013 by Edizioni E/O, translation copyright © 2014 by Europa Editions, published by Europa Editions.

From *A Quiet Belief in Angels* by R.J. Ellory, copyright © R.J. Ellory Publications, Ltd. 2007, published by The Overlook Press, Peter Mayer Publishers, Inc.

From *Gone Girl* by Gillian Flynn, copyright © 2012 by Gillian Flynn, published by Crown Publishers, an imprint of the Crown Publishing Group, a division of Random House LLC.

From *Schroder* by Amity Gaige, copyright © 2013 by Amity Gaige, published by Twelve, an imprint of Grand Central Publishing, a division of Hachette Book Group, Inc.

From *Falling From Horses* by Molly Gloss, copyright © 2014 by Molly Gloss, publishing by Houghton Mifflin Harcourt Publishing Company.

From *Gideon* by Alex Gordon, copyright © 2015 by Alex Gordon, published by Harper Voyager, an imprint of HarperCollins Publishers.

From *The Fault in Our Stars* by John Green, copyright © 2012 by John Green, published by Penguin Group (USA) LLC.

From *The Indian Clerk* by David Leavitt, copyright © 2007 by David Leavitt, published by Bloomsbury USA.

From *Let the Right One In* by John Ajvide Lindqvist, copyright © 2004, translation copyright © 2007 by Ebba Segerberg, published by Thomas Dunne Books, an imprint of St. Martin's Press.

From *Candles on Bay Street* by KC McKinnon, copyright © 1999 by KC McKinnon, published by Doubleday Books.

From *Bloody Jack* by L.A. Meyer, copyright © 2002 by L.A. Meyer, published in the United States by Harcourt Children's Books, an imprint of Houghton Mifflin Harcourt Publishing Company.

From *Twilight* by Stephenie Meyer, copyright © 2005 by Stephenie Meyer, published by Little, Brown and Company, Hachette Book Group USA.

From *The Husband's Secret* by Liane Moriarty, copyright © 2013 by Liane Moriarty, published by The Berkley Publishing Group, the Penguin Group (USA) LLC, a Penguin Random House Company.

From *The Summer of You* by Kate Noble, copyright © 2010 by Kate Noble, published by Berkley Sensation, The Berkley Publishing Group, a division of Penguin Group (USA) Inc.

From *The Sympathizer* by Viet Thanh Nguyen, copyright © 2015 by Viet Thanh Nguyen, published by Grove Press, an imprint of Grove Atlantic.

From *The Watchmaker of Filigree Street* by Natasha Pulley, copyright © 2015 by Natasha Pulley, published by Bloomsbury USA, an imprint of Bloomsbury Publishing Plc.

From *The Silver Linings Playbook* by Matthew Quick, copyright © 2008 by Matthew Quick, publishing by Sarah Crichton Books, an imprint of Farrar, Straus and Giroux.

INDEX

THE EMOTIONAL CRAFT OF FICTION